5 VIEWS ON YOUTH MINISTRY SHORT-TERM MISSIONS
Are Your Trips Helping or Hurting?

Mark Oestreicher, General Editor
Contributors:
Todd Freneaux
Susie Gamez
Jon Huckins
Shawn Kiger
Jim Noreen
Kurt Rietema

5 VIEWS ON YOUTH MINISTRY SHORT-TERM MISSIONS

Copyright © 2020 by The Youth Cartel

Publisher: Mark Oestreicher
Managing Editor: Sarah Hauge
Cover Design: Adam McLane
Layout: Marilee R. Pankratz
Creative Director: Dr. Livingstone, I presume

ISBN-13: 978-1-942145-49-3

The Youth Cartel, LLC
www.theyouthcartel.com
Email: info@theyouthcartel.com
Born in San Diego.
Printed worldwide.

CONTENTS

INTRODUCTION

MARK OESTREICHER

Short-term mission trips are the best and the worst things we do in North American youth ministry.

Let me back up a bit before I unpack that.

While I'm certainly not the oldest person still actively involved in youth ministry, I'm getting up there. Math isn't my strong suit, but I think it's been about thirty-nine years now (the last twenty-one of those at my current church, where I work with the junior high ministry). I haven't been on as many short-term mission trips as my friend Danny Kwon (who wrote The Youth Cartel's fantastic books *Mission Tripping: A Comprehensive Guide to Youth Ministry Missions*, and *Mission Tripping—an Interactive Journal*), who's logged well over fifty trips. That sure is a lot of trips for someone who doesn't work for a short-term missions organization! My memory is a little blurry ('cause I'm old—did I mention that?), but I think my count is roughly twenty-five trips.

On top of that, I've served on the board of a short-term missions organization. And these last two decades, I've been in roles (first at Youth Specialties, and now with The Youth Cartel) where I've both observed the "players" and dialogued with thousands of youth workers about their trip experiences with at least a hundred different short-term missions organizations.

I don't tell you that to start this book with some sort of resume. Instead, I write that to say: I've had an awful lot of input that has informed my extremely strong opinions and beliefs about youth ministry short-term missions (which will be referred to interchangeably as STMs in this book).

I Took My First Trip Because I Was Told Not To

When I was a young youth worker (back in the middle ages), I was an active part of a local youth ministry network in my city. The core of that group included about ten of us, and there were some serious heavy-hitter youth workers in that group whom I looked up to with admiration and aspiration. All of them were focused on high school ministry, and I was the only young guy, and the only person focused on junior high ministry. I felt kinda like a little brother or a mascot amongst them, and lapped up everything they said. I wanted to emulate them. I wanted to grow up and *be like* them.

One day at a gathering of this group, we were talking about short-term missions, and I mentioned that I was wondering what it would be like to take my junior highers on a short-term trip. This was in the early 1980s, and I'm pretty sure no missions groups were offering trips for junior highers at that point—I didn't know anyone who had done a junior high STM (though that could have merely been ignorance on my part). But when I mentioned this idea, my heroes around the table strongly and unanimously told me that short-term missions should be reserved for high schoolers, and that I would be absolutely wrong to take my group on any sort of STM.

I remember this so clearly, because it was in that moment this collection of youth ministry superstars became human in my eyes. Because they were wrong—and I knew it.

The next year, I fumbled my way through a trip to a Native American church in Northern Minnesota with a group of a dozen junior highers (I literally could not find an organization to take us at that time, so I just reached out to a mission church in my denomination and asked if we could come help). I'm sure we did tons of things wrong. But I also saw the impact on my young teens and through my young teens.

My Worst Trip Ever
For a number of years, I loaded teenagers (specifically young teens, since I was a junior high pastor) into vans, and spent weekends at local city missions, and weeks in urban centers and cross-cultural contexts. We started taking junior highers to Mexico—driving twenty-four hours each way from Omaha—and that trip became the centerpiece of our summer programming. We prepped those kids like crazy, even requiring a weekend-long Mission Trip Prep Retreat.

After a few years, someone from my denomination asked if we would open up our trip to other youth groups from around the nation, and about six or seven other churches joined us. They all brought high school groups, and we were there with a big group of junior highers. I went in nervous that our little kids wouldn't have the impact of the other, older groups, and that it would be obvious to everyone, including my group. But just the opposite was true: Most of the other groups were there for what I could only call "ministry tourism." They were there to do a tiny bit of work for the poor and wretched people (please read that with sarcasm) of the village we visited, and to feel better about themselves in the process. Evening debriefs were full of sympathy-tears and pity-projections, but I knew those high schoolers were going home unchanged, and that we'd actually done damage—in the colonialism sense—to the beautiful brothers and sisters we were theoretically serving. Honestly, it sucked. And as the person putting together the trip, I felt responsible.

I knew it was time to do some deeper thinking. I'd grown up with missionary parents (who worked in a mission agency home office), and had good access to people and other sources of great missiology.

And all these years later, that's what this book is at heart: a youth ministry missiology book. Missiology, if you're not familiar with the word, is simply the study of Christian missions, particularly in terms of how methods and purposes are informed by theology, beliefs, worldviews, and assumptions.

Why 5 Views?
A few years back, The Youth Cartel decided to publish a line of "4 Views" books. The similar series I was aware of were mostly focused on theological debate. Our idea was to create a line of books that offered thoughtful *but practical* dialogue about issues in youth ministry. We knew the issues had to be topics youth workers wanted help on, but on which experts in the field disagreed.

We also made a commitment (to ourselves, really) that these books would be written by in-the-trenches youth workers *doing* what they wrote about, rather than experts with opinions, but little to no experience.

Our first book in this line was *4 Views on Pastoring LGBTQ Teenagers*. And the second was *4 Views on Talking to Teenagers About Sex*. Both of those books, and this one, focus on topics that wonderful and thoughtful youth workers disagree on. In all three cases (the first two books and this one), there are plenty of youth workers who didn't or don't realize there's even anything to disagree about! But that's part of the point here: These issues matter greatly, and we want our tribe to be more intentional.

Just when I was wrestling with how to articulate the different "views" for this book so I could pursue writers, I received a book proposal from Kurt Rietema, one of the contributors to this book. He was proposing a book about youth ministry short-term missions as "privilege alleviation." I was super intrigued by his thinking and impressed with his articulation, and knew this had to be one of the views. So, my notes to myself for the five views (before we had any contributors other than Kurt) were:

1. The way most youth min STMs are done these days (work camp approach)
2. Focusing on developing long-term partnership with Indigenous church leaders and serving under their direction
3. Why urban trips are so important, and why they can be so horribly bad
4. "Privilege Alleviation" (Kurt's view)
5. Being shaped for mission, rather than going on a mission trip

Those five concepts, based on the contributors' core commitments and worldviews (really, their missiology), have been shaped by five fantastic practitioners, all of whom I respect deeply, and have become:

1. A Holistic Approach to Work Camps (Todd Freneaux)
2. Developing Long-Term Partnerships with Indigenous Church Leaders (Jim Noreen)
3. Approaching Urban Missions as Life-Long Learners,

Advocates, and Allies (Susie Gamez)
4. Alleviating Privilege through Short-Term Missions (Kurt Rietema)
5. From Charity to Solidarity: Decolonizing Short-Term Missions (Jon Huckins)

As with our previous books in this line, each of the contributors also offers a short response to one of the other views, creating something of a dialogue.

OH, and somewhere along the line, I thought we needed a couple of specific issues addressed, and we added two short appendices: one on the uniqueness of trips with junior highers (written by Todd Freneaux), and one on multigenerational mission trips (written by Shawn Kiger).

Back to My Opening Statement

I still believe, quite strongly, that short-term missions are the best and the worst things we do in North American youth ministry (my "North American" qualifier there is due to the fact that youth min STMs have become something of a cottage industry in the U.S., and are often approached *very* differently, if at all, in other countries).

In fact, I'd go as far as saying that the majority of youth ministry short-term missions are problematic, at least partially. They may have some value for the participants, but they often inadvertently teach bad theology and worldviews that are more about imperialism than the kingdom of God.

But, when done well, with thoughtfulness, humility, and an informed missiology, all recipients can benefit in profound ways that build up the kingdom. I chose "all recipients" very intentionally in that previous sentence, as the best STMs are not about us who go as "givers" and those we visit as "receivers." Instead, we are all receiving, and hopefully experiencing something that smells a little like heaven. We hope this book nudges you in that direction.

Marko

VIEW 1:
A HOLISTIC APPROACH
TO WORK CAMPS

BY TODD FRENEAUX

INTRODUCTION

When I was a teenager in youth group, my church never provided an opportunity for us to go on a short-term mission trip. Truthfully, I never even knew what a mission trip was until I returned to the church a few years later to volunteer as one of the leaders for the youth group.

I lived close to Washington, DC, in northern Virginia, and I remember struggling with why there were so many homeless men and women living on the streets there. I was a starry-eyed twenty-something who wanted answers as to why things were the way they were so that I could change the world, of course.

It was the 1980s and there was a lot of press about the homeless in the nation's capital. I decided to go into Washington, DC, on a very cold winter day to get an up-close look at what was happening. I was hungry for answers and very interested in what life was like on the streets. I took a tape recorder and interviewed several homeless men and women. Standing around a fifty-five-gallon drum that contained a roaring fire, I listened while three or four of these men spoke freely about their lives. I remember wanting to spend that night on the streets to see what it was like. I came very close to doing so but chickened out at the last minute.

I discovered a lot that day. There were many sad stories of people who had been dealt a bad hand in life. Depression, drugs, alcohol, and other addictions played a large role. I could not have articulated it back then, but what I saw was a lot of brokenness and hopelessness. At one point I interviewed homeless advocate Mitch Snyder, with the DC-based Community for Creative Non-Violence. He was almost single-handedly responsible for all the attention around the issue of homelessness in Washington at the time. Because of his radical methods (hunger strikes, chaining himself to the White House fence, etc.) he also garnered a great deal of support and was very successful in getting a lot done for those living on the streets. I really admired his passion and commitment to help people who had few possessions and no place to lay their heads at night. Mitch was blunt, telling me at one point that I should leave my job, sell all my possessions, move to the city, and work for him, where I could make a "real difference."

I didn't. But he got me thinking: What could we do in the church with the youth group to make a difference in the world?

I knew enough about the Bible back then to know that it was full of commands to care for the poor and needy, and the blessings that come to those who share and show compassion to those who are suffering.

> *The generous will themselves be blessed, for they share their food with the poor.* (Proverbs 22:9)

> *"For I was hungry, and you gave me something to eat, I was thirsty, and you gave me something to drink, I was a stranger and you invited me in."* (Matthew 25:35)

And I was equally familiar with many verses that served as a warning to those who ignore those in need.

> *Whoever shuts their ears to the cry of the poor will also cry out and not be answered.* (Proverbs 21:13)

*If anyone has material possessions and sees a brother or sister in
need but has no pity on them, how can the love of God be in that
person? Dear children, let us not love with words or speech but with
actions and in truth.* (1 John 3:17-18)

Soon after my trip into the city, with a newfound excitement to help
those in need and a desire to be obedient to God's word, I researched
student missions organizations looking for an opportunity for the
youth group where I was volunteering, and eventually decided on
a week-long mission trip to the Appalachian region. I presented
the idea of going to the church staff person who oversaw the youth
program and she was equally excited. "Let's do it!" she said, followed
quickly by, "You're in charge." She was very supportive but allowed
me to work out the details and lead the trip. I was so pumped about
this new thing we were doing to help people, and excited about
introducing teenagers to the concept of serving others.

That summer, we took a small group of high school students and the
trip was really great. We worked on homes and helped those who
simply didn't have the resources to address some of the basic needs
to ensure their homes were safe and dry. There was a lot of poverty in
the region where we served and we were all amazed that people lived
in such terrible conditions. After all, we were upper-middle-class
white adult leaders and teenagers from northern Virginia who had
pretty much everything we wanted. We were completely oblivious to
the way many people in the world lived. The trip opened our eyes to
the needs of the poor, many of whom didn't have things we took for
granted every day, like a dry home, solid floors, or functional steps to
safely enter and exit their house. We did some good work that really
helped people. It was also hard work, but we had a great time serving
together as a youth group.

The next summer, we did it again. And the summer after that. And
the summer after that.

Many years later as the full-time director of youth ministries in a
large, traditional United Methodist church, it was my practice to
work with a different missions organization each year. At that point in

my ministry, we were doing both spring break and summer mission trips. I began introducing my teenagers to other types of missions opportunities, such as serving the homeless in inner city Washington, DC, and educating teens about domestic and global hunger issues through a gleaning ministry. Every fourth year we would go to Mexico for a cross-cultural experience.

I loved mission trips. I loved the impact they had on those we served and those who served, and I loved seeing how in one week we could make huge improvements in people's quality of life. I loved moving teenagers out of their self-centered worlds and giving them opportunities to look beyond themselves and truly serve others, selflessly. I loved knowing that we were doing as Jesus instructed us to do: care for the poor.

But as much as I loved mission trips, there was still something missing.

MY PRIORITIES

PRIORITY #1: A HOLISTIC APPROACH

For many years, I was content with doing these week-long home-repair mission trips. But I wasn't mature enough in my faith to identify spiritual formation as the missing crucial ingredient. My focus was on social justice and that's all that mattered to me. Thankfully, my thinking evolved.

In 1997, I and two other youth pastors founded the Jeremiah Project, which began out of a need to provide a short-term mission trip specifically designed for junior high participants. We used the work camp approach, meaning that teens travel from out of town or out of state for a week of service with their youth group, working during the day and then participating in some type of program or activity in the evening. The other ministry founders and I discovered that very few missions organizations wanted anything to do with this amazing age group. There were tons of mission trip experiences for senior high students, but very few for junior high.

When we founded the Jeremiah Project, we were passionate about building a missions ministry with a holistic approach. In other words, this means that in the planning and execution of all aspects of the mission trip experience, service and spiritual formation are inseparable. They are equally important, working in tandem to bring about real transformation in the lives of those who serve *and* those we are serving.

Conversely, I believe that many missions organizations have a fragmented approach to missions work. When considering service and spiritual formation, they treat them as two separate elements, rather than seeing each one as needing the other in order to be effective. All too often the service component becomes the main priority while the emphasis on spiritual formation is minimal, or worse, nonexistent. Under this model, success seems to be measured by how many projects are completed, how quickly the work gets done, and how great the finished product is (lots of before and after pictures).

Don't get me wrong, I'm all for making homes warmer, safer, drier, and more accessible. After all, that's certainly what we do each summer through our ministry. It's taken me a long time to get this, but what I've come to understand is that just repairing homes is not enough! And let's face it; there are a ton of existing regional and national nonprofits that repair homes all day long, and do a much better job than many faith-based ministries can.

Still, some would argue that the mark of a successful mission trip is repairing homes, coupled with the feeling of satisfaction one gets by helping other people. I disagree. Mission trips should change people's lives. And while feelings are nice, they don't change lives. A new set of front steps is great, but it improves the quality of someone's life for a relatively short period of time. An encounter with *God* is what changes lives and brings about real, long-term transformation.

A Holistic Approach...*for Those We Serve*
When I talk about a holistic approach for those we serve, I am saying that whenever possible we need to strive to meet the physical, social,

and spiritual needs of each person we serve, viewing each of those components as equally important and inseparable.

Upon our leadership team's initial visit with an individual (or family) who has requested our services, we try to be very sensitive to the needs demonstrated. We listen carefully for signs that give us insight into their spoken and unspoken needs.

Physical Needs

Clearly, one of our goals is to meet the physical needs of each person, and in our organization we do this by performing repairs on their home. Meeting very real physical needs is vitally important. Summer after summer, I witness the significant impact these efforts have on improving the quality of life for individuals. What a joy it is to see someone gain full access to their home for the first time since becoming wheelchair bound. What a privilege it is to be part of an organization that provides a roof over a porch so that a woman dying of emphysema can enjoy her remaining days sitting outside, watching the birds on beautiful mornings. What a gift it is to provide a new, sturdy set of low-rise steps so that an elderly couple can safely enter and exit their home. What a blessing it is that a work team can spend a day at a mobile home and fix a roof that has been leaking for *years*. This is amazing stuff, and I believe it pleases the heart of God when we care for his children in such tangible ways.

Social Needs

For some, the social need is evident: They have no family nearby or they simply don't have any family at all. Even for those who do have family nearby, sometimes those family members never come by to visit. The reality is that for some folks, we represent the most social interaction they will have *all year long*. Wow. Let that sink in for a moment. These folks are *desperate* for human interaction, for company and conversation. Many of those individuals are very lonely and just want someone to talk to, or they are craving human touch because no one ever hugs them or puts their arm around them to show affection. For some, meeting this very basic human need is equal to, or more important than, any repairs we could perform at their home.

It's not uncommon for us to spend time with people year after year who don't have any significant home repair needs. Their biggest need is social, and that's okay. Actually, it's more than okay, it's a blessing.

Paul reminds us to take time to do the simple things for others:

> *Therefore, as we have opportunity, let us do good to all people...* (Galatians 6:10)

Spiritual Needs

Finally, there are the spiritual needs we try to meet. For a host of reasons, this is hard for some people in missions work to prioritize. But it's important, because every person our ministry has ever encountered has had the same need as you and I: to have a personal relationship with God through Jesus Christ. There are some we serve who know Jesus, and some who do not. I believe we need to be about the business of tending to physical homes *as well as* spiritual homes when the opportunities present themselves.

The prevailing thought in missiology emphasizes that we meet the physical needs of those we serve and maybe some of the social needs, but nothing more. But I would argue that we also have a *responsibility* to engage in conversations of faith with those we serve and to be prepared to share the hope that we have.

> *...Always be prepared to give an answer to everyone who asks you to give the reason for the hope that you have...* (1 Peter 3:15)

Throughout Scripture, we see Jesus tending to the physical needs of those who come to him to be healed. And though there may not be Scripture to support the details of every encounter, I cannot ever imagine Jesus simply meeting a person's physical needs without also addressing their most important need—to know God.

A Two-Way Street

I would be remiss if I did not mention the importance of those we serve having the opportunity to share their faith with *us*. This is huge. We tend to think that we are going to share our faith with those less fortunate and assume that because they are poor in material things, they are not rich in spiritual things. This couldn't be further from the truth. I look for and welcome opportunities for those we serve to share their faith journeys with our teenagers. This is another way God wants to use the setting of a mission trip to glorify himself!

I recall an older gentleman whom I will refer to as Mr. Smith. From the moment I met Mr. Smith, he couldn't stop talking about Jesus, his need for a Savior, and his life's journey, which had required him to fully rely on God. With each visit, I'd pull up a chair and listen intently to his stories of faith. His was an amazing story anybody could relate to and be blessed by. We would always end our time in prayer, and I would listen as Mr. Smith shared his gratitude for our assistance and praised God for our paths crossing. Before I left, I would always encourage him to share his faith with the teens coming to his home that summer. He needed no invitation, but it was my way of giving him permission to do so since they were "youngsters" (his word).

Over the next several weeks as groups worked on Mr. Smith's home, youth and adults would come back to camp and talk about their time with him. Through his testimony, they learned about what it really means to rely on God for everything. "Better than my pastor's sermons," quipped one eighth grade boy about what Mr. Smith shared with them.

Embracing the responsibility of sharing Jesus with those we serve and intentionally engaging in conversations of faith changes our whole approach to missions work. I'm not saying it's easy or that we do this consistently. We have hundreds of teens and adults serving each summer and each one is in a different place in their walk with Christ. What we need to remember, though, is what Jesus makes quite clear in John 15:5: "apart from me, you can do nothing." That's true individually, and as a missions organization. We will be only bear fruit when we remain connected to the one true vine.

A Holistic Approach...*for Those Who Are Serving*
We know that teenagers sign up for mission trips for a variety of

reasons, but for many it is because somewhere along the line they were taught that Christians should serve this way as an outgrowth of their faith. "Jesus served others, so we should be serving others," the youth leader teaches. That's good, and it's theologically correct.

The problem is, that reason for serving doesn't necessarily result in an individual developing a servant's heart, or in continued impact for the kingdom of God. When people do things driven solely by obligation, it can be effective in the short term, but the motivation usually wanes over time.

But what if teens were driven by something other than *obligation*? What if they were driven to serve because they experienced a personal encounter with Jesus that totally changed their lives, and they couldn't help but want to love and serve others as a result? What if their motivation to serve was that their hearts were broken for the things that break God's heart? And what if teens fell in love with this Jesus who promises that if you'll just stay connected to him, you will produce fruit (John 15:5)? Here's what would happen: We would see a generation of teenagers who remain passionate servants for the kingdom of God long after the mission trip ends. And we would train up an army of believers who no longer see service as a project but as a way of life. A fruit-bearing life does not easily fade. It is not based on feelings but remains because of a deep connection to, and a love for, God.

Mission trips provide amazing opportunities for lives to change.

Think about this for a moment: Why do we take our teenagers away for weekend retreats? We do this so they can come away, or "retreat," and withdraw from the world's distractions, so they can live in Christian community, and so they can encounter God in ways that aren't really possible one night a week at youth group. We do weekend retreats because we know they are effective.

I believe the opportunity is even *greater* on a week-long mission trip. Picture this: You have a bunch of junior high students who are going away for a week-long mission trip because they think it will be fun, or their friend convinced them to go, or they just want to be away from home for a while, or their youth leader told them they should go, or (fill in the blank). Admittedly, some don't have any idea why they signed up and are completely clueless. Isn't that awesome?

After the initial shock of "Why the heck am I here?" wears off, teens slowly become more comfortable and start making friends. They settle into the routine of getting up, having morning devotions, going to the worksite, playing games, and then having fun at the evening program.

As each day goes by, teens begin to shed the façade of trying to be cool, or they stop pretending to be someone they're not. Why? Because they're in this safe, Christian community, where they begin to realize they can just be themselves.

At the worksite, the teen who has never picked up a hammer takes five minutes to drive a single nail into the board. One of the adults on the site knows the importance of empowering this person instead of overpowering him, and patiently teaches him how to better accomplish this task. By the end of the day this young man is no longer taking five minutes to drive a nail, he's doing it in five *seconds*. The smile that comes over him is priceless. He is beginning to realize that he can make a difference and it eventually dawns on him that God is actually using him right now!

At the evening program, youth have the opportunity to share where they saw God during the day, which moves from silly comments the first part of the week to profound moments with deep insight by the week's end. They have learned to recognize God's activity around them.

And then for some, their hearts become tender to the messages each night and something inside them changes. Their hearts turn to God and the singing is no longer just singing. It becomes worship.

By the end of the week, youth who didn't know why they were on this mission trip in the first place find themselves overcome with emotion as they realize it's time to go home. But they leave knowing that God has a plan for them, that they are not too young to make a difference, and that they are loved by the One who created them.

When teenagers come for a week to serve others, it presents a unique and amazing opportunity. We want teens to have the opportunity to serve others and to be part of something bigger than themselves as they work to make homes warmer, safer, drier, and more accessible for those in need. But we also want to encourage young believers to go deeper in their faith as well as to point non-believers toward a life-changing relationship with God through Jesus Christ.

PRIORITY #2: PEOPLE OVER PROJECTS

It was probably around 4 p.m. on my third day in wild, wonderful West Virginia. I had been meeting with five to six families and individuals each day to share about our ministry, get a glimpse into their world, and determine if we could meet the home-repair needs they requested us to fill later that summer during our work camps. I love this time, but as an introvert, I also find it totally exhausting. Listening to their stories was, many times, heartbreaking. By this point in the late afternoon I was totally drained and looking forward to some alone time that evening to decompress. But that all changed with a single phone call from a woman named Ms. Kim.

Ms. Kim told me she was in need of a wheelchair ramp. She wanted me to determine whether one of our groups could do that project, and asked if I could come out to take a look—today. In my head I was reluctant because I was so done, but, thankfully, the words that came out of my mouth were, "Sure, I can do that." She gave me her address and I hung up. After putting the address into my GPS, I discovered that it would be a thirty-minute drive to her house. I let out a big sigh and then pointed the truck down the long, windy mountain road heading into nowhere-land.

After fifteen minutes of driving along West Virginia mountain roads, I began to complain to myself. "What an inconvenience this is. I should have never answered the phone." What a rotten attitude for the leader of a missions organization to have, right? Yes it was, as God would soon convict me.

I pulled up to a mobile home with a front deck that looked as though it could come crashing down with nothing more than a gentle nudge. As I made my way up the rickety steps I was greeted with a smile from a woman in a wheelchair. "You must be Todd!" she exclaimed as she extended her hand. "Yes, and you must be Ms. Kim," I responded. "I am," she said, followed by, "You look like you've had a hard day. Can I pray for you?" I was taken aback by her question. I totally didn't see that one coming. A lump welled up in my throat as I felt humbled and ashamed at the same time. "Yes," I replied. "That's just what I need."

When she finished praying for me, she began to tell me her situation. Wheelchair-bound, she was living alone and had no access out of her home. Every time she needed to see her doctor or shop for food, her elderly neighbor would come and carry her down the rotting steps. Despite her challenges, Ms. Kim had a peace and joy about her, for which she quickly gave credit to Jesus.

She talked about how great being able to get in and out of her home with a wheelchair ramp would be. As I listened, my own words of how "inconvenienced" I was by having to drive thirty minutes at the end of a long day echoed shamefully in my head. I had no idea what it meant to be inconvenienced. God has this way of correcting his children when we need it. Wow, what a blessing our time together was. We prayed and said goodbye and I told Ms. Kim that we would see her that summer.

Our teams spent several weeks replacing her deck and building her a wheelchair ramp. Was that physical work important? Absolutely. Ms. Kim could now safely access her home, all by herself. But every day, teams came back from her house not talking about how fun and meaningful it was to build a ramp, but instead talking about getting to know Ms. Kim, listening to her stories, hearing her talk about Jesus, and praying. Every day they expressed what a blessing *she* was to *them*.

Ever since the day I met Ms. Kim, I have looked at those we serve very differently. I no longer see them as potential projects; I now see them as people to love and be loved by.

More recently, there's the story of Mr. Hill. For many years our teams worked on Mr. Hill's home, way out in the sticks on the outskirts of Winchester, Virginia. He was ninety-something and lived alone with no family nearby. His wife had passed away about five years earlier. Each spring he would call us and in his raspy voice leave a detailed voicemail listing all the projects he needed done that summer—"if you have the time," he would always add. He would also type a letter on his antique 1920s typewriter and mail me a copy, just to make sure I had a record of his requests.

Mr. Hill's projects were usually not very involved: yardwork, painting, installing a new post for his bird feeder, repairing some lattice that the local bears had damaged on his porch, and so on. But his real need was for someone to talk to. Oh, how he loved having teens come out to his home to visit. What joy it brought him to hear laughter and share lunch with these young people. He looked forward to it every summer.

Then one spring not long ago, he was diagnosed with cancer. When I came to visit him in May I noticed that he had lost some weight from the previous year, weight he could not afford to lose. As usual, we had plans for our teams to spend a week or so there doing some odd jobs, cutting his grass, etc. Over the summer his health began to decline rapidly.

One day he called and asked if I could come by and connect his IV to his bag of nutritional supplement because he couldn't secure the connection. I did, and began coming by almost every day so he could get his twice-daily dose of Ensure. Some of the adults who were on the work team at his home would assist with this task and other simple medical needs. Eventually, Mr. Hill became so weak that he could not easily get out of bed to answer the door, so he just left it unlocked for me and others to come in. He was also too weak to get dressed, and I usually found him clothed only in a diaper, which barely stayed in place due to his emaciated condition.

His daughter lived in New England and was having difficulty getting time off to come see her father. I called and told her she really needed to be there to care for her dad, as I couldn't be available as frequently as he needed me. She did eventually come to care for him, and this allowed me to visit when I could work it into my schedule. Toward the end, I became more intentional about steering the conversation with Mr. Hill toward faith and Jesus. He was not a believer and his daughter and I both knew this. She had spent many years sharing Jesus with him, but he was an intellectual who simply could not embrace this idea about needing a Savior. He respected Jesus as a teacher and wise man, but not as his Savior. Despite this, I shared about my need for Jesus and what he had done in my life, and always prayed with Mr. Hill before I left.

Mr. Hill died not long after that summer's work camps had ended. I attended his small graveside service with my summer intern. There were no more than ten of us there. At the service, I reflected on the time we had spent with Mr. Hill over the years and I was reminded once again that people are more important than projects. He really didn't care about the little things we did around his home. What meant the most to him was being known and loved by those who came to spend time with him.

During one of my last visits with Mr. Hill, he expressed the joy it brought him to have us there each summer. He said, "You know, there's something special and different about you, your organization, and the kids who visit me each year, and I know God has something to do with that." Yes, he does.

When we dare to really invest in relationships with those we serve, something special happens. There's a connection that can take place that far exceeds our expectations. I believe this, too, pleases the heart of God.

MY APPROACH

Over the years, our leaders have established several non-negotiables when it comes to our work camp mission trips. These are anchors that keep us focused and bear substantial fruit within our work camp setting. What follows are just a few of our eight core values.

Personal

"Bigger is better" doesn't apply to our mission trips. We intentionally keep our camps small. We believe that ministry happens at a deep level when teenagers experience program and worship in a small group setting. We want to get to know junior high students and call them by name. We never want any of them to feel like they are just a number. We place a high value on young teenagers being known and feeling a sense of belonging in our setting.

Leadership

Our staff leadership model is unique in that we have new staff every week of the summer. We want our staff to be fresh, energetic, and excited for the entire week to ensure that we are giving the teenagers and their leaders our very best.

As part of the staff leadership team, we primarily select youth pastors to serve as program directors (speakers) for the week. We want the teaching of God's word to come from a more spiritually mature voice. And we work hard at selecting excellent communicators to keep teenagers and adults engaged each night.

Faith

Moving teens to a deeper relationship with Christ is one of the priorities I mentioned earlier. So, how do we as a ministry do that? First, we are very intentional about the spiritual formation of our campers. It starts with beginning to pray six to eight months in advance of our summer work camps and seeking God's leading for the summer theme. What truths does God want us to share with teenagers this summer? What memory verse does he want us to teach teens so that they can hide his word in their hearts (Psalm 119:11)?

Once the vision is cast, a design team spends one to two months praying and planning the details of the daily program before inviting other program directors to contribute their ideas. Once that is complete, we start preparing the details for the summer.

Each day of camp provides an opportunity for participants to practice healthy, life-giving, spiritual habits. We begin every morning with devotions that end with about ten minutes of quiet time. After lunch at the work site, we reinforce the daily Scripture and theme for the day as work teams discuss the Scripture, read an accompanying story that relates to the theme, and take turns responding to the small group questions we provide.

Our evening program (which lasts about an hour and a half) is designed specifically for our audience: young teens. This time is fun and fast-paced and is packed with music, games, activities, small groups, video clips, worship, the Word, a relevant and engaging message, and more. Youth are learning and growing every night, and they look forward to this time.

Participants are also given opportunities every night to share the ways in which they see God moving in their lives or in the lives of others. We also set aside one of the nights later in the week for an invitation—an opportunity to respond to what God may be stirring up in their hearts.

How do I know this approach is effective? There are several markers.

One is the higher-than-normal retention rate among churches. Approximately 85 percent of churches that experience our summer missions camps return every year. They see the impact it has on their youth, their adult leaders, their youth group, and their church.

Another is the fact that in any given summer, about 80 percent of our staff is comprised of former campers. A mission trip can leave an indelible mark on a young person's life and draw them back time and time again.

Finally, and most importantly, are the thousands of lives that have been changed. I witness this up close and personally each summer. We receive further evidence through the applications of former Jeremiah Project participants once they become old enough to apply to be on our staff, like this one from an eleventh grader:

"I participated in the Jeremiah Project as a middle schooler and it completely changed my life. Going into my first year, I didn't believe in God, I just went because my mom wanted me to. One week later, leaving the camp, I had absolutely no doubt that God was real, and the best part was, I knew he was on my side. That 'knowing' feeling has never gone away."

One twelfth grader shared about her faith-changing experience as a junior higher. *"The third day of camp, I had a long conversation with one of the homeowners. She talked to me about how happy and thankful she was for us to be there. I felt this very weird shiver go through me, and I asked her if we could pray together. Now I know that the shiver was the Holy Spirit, and I feel the shiver all the time. That prayer changed my life…if it wasn't for this experience, I don't know where my relationship with God would be today."*

This is the type of transformation that can happen when we place Christ at the center of a week of missions. Of course, it doesn't happen for every teen, but I know seeds are planted and God doesn't waste any opportunity when we are faithful to share his Word.

> *"…so is my word that goes out from my mouth: It will not return to me empty, but will accomplish what I desire and achieve the purpose for which I sent it."* (Isaiah 55:11)

Community

Our ministry's goal from day one has been to remain long-term in the communities we serve. Except for one location, we have held true to that for twenty-two years. Why is that important? Without an ongoing presence in these communities, we are unable to build relationships and trust with those we serve. Although we serve new people each summer, there are many we serve repeatedly over the years. This helps us do more in the lives of folks than just fix their homes, moving us from an "organization to client" relationship to a "friend to friend" or a "brother or sister in Christ" relationship. It's these relationships that sometimes result in deeper conversations about life and faith. Out of the depths of these relationships come invitations to attend graduations, weddings, or other family events. Hospital visits, and even some requests to attend or speak at funerals, are not uncommon.

Members of our team also send personalized Christmas cards each year to everyone we served the previous summer. We receive many in return, attached to notes of appreciation for our presence and for the work we did.

During each mission trip week, Thursday night is our banquet. It is one of my favorite nights. Earlier in the week we begin inviting those we are serving to come to camp, where we will be hosting a banquet and they will be our special guests. We usually decorate the dining hall with white tablecloths and add some nice touches like candles, balloons, and streamers. Sometimes we have two or three folks join us for dinner while other times we have twelve or more. These banquets are opportunities for us to share a meal with our new friends outside of the work setting, to serve them a great meal, and to engage in a time of fellowship.

For me, it's a glimpse of heaven as I see people who were strangers not long ago now breaking bread together, laughing, telling stories, and sharing life. I believe heaven and earth touch each Thursday night. After dinner, some families will stay for more conversation and even stick around for our evening program, participating in worship and listening to the message. Pretty cool.

FINAL THOUGHTS

I was visiting a friend in New York recently when her husband asked me what I did for a living. Apparently, my eyes lit up as I began to share all about our ministry and what I have the privilege of doing every summer. After a few minutes of sharing he interrupted me with an observation. "You have said several times that you love your job. That's really special," he said. "I can't truthfully say the same about my job. Why do you love it so much?" I told him that it's quite simple: I have the best of both worlds. I get to help people in need and at the same time help youth develop servants' hearts and point them toward Jesus.

I love short-term mission trips. The impact they have on those we serve and those who come to serve continues to amaze me. Best of all is witnessing firsthand the power of God transforming lives, seeing his kingdom come and his will being done on earth as it is in heaven.

RESPONSE

SUSIE GAMEZ

I love that last story. Wouldn't it be amazing if we all loved what we did so much that our eyes would light up whenever we talked about our work? The idea of "loving what you do" often feels like a luxury for a select few, and while in reality that may be the case, I think if more of us were truly living out our God-given purpose, there would also be a lot more of us who could honestly say we love what we do.

Thank you for this insightful chapter, Todd. It's encouraging and refreshing to see that you are not overlooking the capacity and potential in young people, particularly junior high students. I believe their experience with the Jeremiah Project will lay a foundation that normalizes a life of learning from and serving others. What great discipleship and leadership training!

The way that you highlighted the reciprocal nature of relationships especially resonated with me. I am skeptical of folks who do not seek to learn from others—particularly when the well-resourced assume they know better than the under-resourced. The prayers of Ms. Kim are memorable and powerful. The way teens would share about how much they learned from Mr. Smith is a good example of how much we have to learn from those who are different from us. It also speaks to the "upside down" nature of the kingdom of God. The young person who said that conversations with Mr. Smith were "better than my pastor's sermons!" proves the point that positions and titles sometimes have little to do with whom God will use to bring him glory.

One thing I did find a bit lacking was discussion on how you might prepare teenagers for the cross-cultural elements of this trip. Given the two geographical demographics, I am assuming (perhaps incorrectly) that both those serving with the Jeremiah Project and those who are being served are mostly white. Despite the fact that they may be part of the same racial group, obviously there are some marked cultural differences between the two groups. Is there any cultural training given to teen participants before they leave home? Any lessons on why the socioeconomic disparities between the community the teenagers come from and the community of the people they will serve exist?

Perhaps a brief historical overview of the area would be helpful in giving the short-term missions participants a greater understanding of how and why the region became so impoverished. Not only will this give them a greater sense of compassion and empathy for the people they serve, I believe it could also lead to a more transformational approach to "loosing the cords of injustice." Perhaps some of these teens will be inspired to pursue a vocational pathway that can help alleviate poverty from a more root-cause level.

Learning about some of the root causes of poverty can also help the non-poor understand how they have benefitted from current systems without their necessarily having shown much merit of their own. Helping youth understand what "privilege" is, how it functions, and how they can leverage their privilege to benefit others should be a part of our discipleship—it is being a faithful steward and part of living out the call to all believers to love our neighbors. This sort of education can also help fight against some of the "god complexes" that emerge from those who come from more privileged backgrounds. A lesson from the beatitudes might be a good springboard for some of these conversations.

Lessons from an "insider expert" or a cultural mentor would also be great things to incorporate. It sounds like this happens organically as you spend time with people like Ms. Kim, Mr. Smith, and Mr. Hill, but how honorable would it be to specifically ask someone like Ms. Kim to serve as, and be regarded as, a mentor to the groups who visit? I imagine it would give her a great sense of pride and it would further ingrain the lesson that the financially non-poor have much to learn from the poor.

I started with praise, then gave some critique, and I will top the sandwich with some more praise. I am so thankful that organizations like the Jeremiah Project exist. Mobilizing God's people (especially young people) to missions is work we are all called to. It is the actionable response to the prayer "thy kingdom come, thy will be done on earth as it is in heaven." Thank you for your faithfulness, and would you continue to faithfully serve until Jesus does in fact return!

VIEW 2:
DEVELOPING LONG-TERM PARTNERSHIPS WITH INDIGENOUS CHURCH LEADERS

BY JIM NOREEN

INTRODUCTION

I was leading a missions team on a dusty Haitian mountainside shortly after the devastating earthquake of 2010. Here I was with ten team members working on a house. It was a Monday, the day the construction aspect of the trip began. The stage had been set to do this well—and I was about to mess it up.

Let me rewind and give you some background on myself, and how I ended up on a mountainside in the Caribbean. I was eighteen when I caught the missions bug. I was on a trip with my youth group to inner-city Vancouver, British Columbia, lodging in a church with dozens of other youth. We served in the surrounding area, working in soup kitchens, food pantries, and the like. Having grown up in North Dakota, this was another world—and I loved it. Not so much Vancouver, but the adventure. The newness. Feeling "needed" and useful. I came back from an experience that had, in many ways, changed my life. It altered my trajectory, and I landed at a Bible college in Minneapolis. At Bible college, I would love to say I was a star student, but I wasn't. The allure of adventure and new experiences drove me, and often distracted me. Each January, our college offered a unique opportunity: You could attend two

weeks of classes on missions, or you could receive the same credit
for participating in a mission trip. That January, I found myself on
a plane to Haiti where I would spend the next month volunteering
with a ministry in the mountains. I returned from that trip with the
same realization many students have after a mission trip: I had no
desire to sit in a classroom. I just wanted to be back in Haiti. With
spring break coming up, I requested two additional weeks of absence
from our dean of students, and six weeks later I was back in Haiti for
another month. Life in the States was good, but the responsibilities of
school, work, and even playing on the college basketball team were
not enough to hold back my craving for adventure. It became evident
that I was given the "gift" of carelessness, in the best sense. Saying yes
to opportunities was a habit. The summer after my freshman year I
traveled the U.S. with a team of three fellow students, working with
local churches and assisting them during their VBS week before
heading to the next church to do the same. This is where my passion
for the local church began. Working with local churches in ten
different cities that summer of college, I saw the similarities shared by
those churches, and witnessed first-hand the consistent power that is
found in passionate, Christ-following congregations.

I returned from that summer and took a step into another adventure.
I got engaged—at nineteen. I returned to school that fall, went to
Haiti again that January, graduated from the two-year school that
spring, and then I was off. I married my wife, we hopped in a car,
and we drove cross-country to a California church I had visited
the summer before. My wife and I spent our first year of marriage
working for a church, serving in children's and youth ministry,
learning and failing along the way. Adventure. We returned to
Minnesota after that year, unable to withstand the cost of the
California life, but with no regrets. I once again engaged in youth
ministry, this time at a local church in the Minneapolis suburbs, and
I also picked up a full-time job in the corporate world. Three years
later, I was looking to take my youth group on their first-ever mission
trip.

The backdrop of my experiences shaped what I was looking for. I had
a passion for the local church, and the power within it. I had a desire

for adventure, but also a desire for connection. I began asking around, speaking my dreams of what I was looking for in our mission trip. I wanted our church to engage in a partnership with a local church in another culture. I wanted to see our church cultivate a relationship where we would return to that same church community year after year. Where we prayed for them, they prayed for us. We learned their stories, they learned ours. I ended up speaking these thoughts to a friend at our church, and through that connection was introduced to a sending organization with the same passions. I signed up our youth group for a trip. Three months into the process, I learned that the sending org, Praying Pelican Missions, was looking for additional staff as they continued to grow. I applied, and as of January 2, 2010, I was on staff. I left my job in the corporate world, reduced to volunteer status at my church, and entered into full-time ministry. I was hired as a base level mission trip leader, recruiting teams, preparing them for their trip, and then leading them on the mission field. Ten days after becoming a staff member, on January 12, 2010, a 7.0 earthquake rocked Haiti.

Three months post-earthquake I was sitting with pastors in Port-au-Prince, Haiti, hearing their stories and asking how we could come alongside them. After the earthquake there was a season of hundreds (maybe thousands?) of missions teams contacting sending organizations and asking how their teams could assist. Our staff was sifting through how to even begin. Our approach was simple— we went directly to local church leadership and asked obvious questions: "How can we help?" "What are the biggest needs in your community?" "How would you use a missions team?"

We learned much through those questions, but as we began to flesh out what teams would actually be doing, it began to seem like we could suggest almost anything and the answer would be "yes." Hearing all the "yeses" from these pastors instilled in me the need to enter into more genuine partnership, where we could have more honest, two-sided conversations. Just receiving a "yes" or "okay" from a pastor as we talked through ideas, concepts, or thoughts often seemed empty and, oftentimes, too easy. I felt like we were consistently walking a line between being taken advantage of, and us being the ones taking advantage of the pastors of these local congregations. My desire was to truly learn each pastor's vision and heart for their community, and then utilize our groups to assist them and fuel these passions. These pastors were hurting, and the last thing I wanted to do was add to the mess.

This desire not to cause harm is shared by all of us, whether we have said it out loud or not. I've never heard a short-term missions leader say they desire to create a mess. Even the most irresponsible trips, more often than not, come about through good intentions. The issue is not that we are in it for the wrong reasons. I truly believe that. The issue lies in the fact that we don't know what we don't know. As we have continued to serve in Haiti, we have naturally discovered ways that we have failed. These failures have led to learning, and valuable knowledge has been gained. However, just when we finally know something, we uncover other areas where we have failed. It's a constant process of refinement. Through it all, this truth has been instilled in me: Failure that comes out of humility, respect, and love is a gift that is met with much grace.

Let's be real. When you are a guest in another culture and community, the community knows that you are clueless. They are ready to give grace as you fumble through learning the culture. Be humble, show respect and love, and you will have the benefit of the doubt granted to you in almost any scenario. This is important to conceptualize, as short-term missions failures are oftentimes used to discourage community-based missions. I encourage leaders to ask questions, advise their teams, and relax on the little things. Know this: If your team enters into a community with humbleness and respect, with the spirit of love as your motive, you will not fail. You will not mess things up in a way that does lasting harm.

So with that said, let's get started. The views I am going to outline are primarily from the context of international missions to global locations where the Christian church has been established in some fashion. Many of the concepts discussed apply domestically as well, but I recognize that much of the discussion (and controversy) on short-term missions revolves around cross-cultural ministry.

Throughout this discussion, I am going to outline why I believe effective missions begin and end with the local church. There's a special calling that is only found within the local congregation, and when missions are used to fuel that calling, I believe God does incredible things.

MY PRIORITIES

The Local Church

This strong emphasis on the local church is due to the truth that the local church is the catalyst for reaching the world for Christ. We all know, or should know, that our missions teams are not bringing Jesus to our missions locations. He is already there, working through the hands and feet of local believers. It is within these groups of believers that his fire is burning. These local believers have the context of their culture, they have established relationships, and they have a vested interest in the mission, unlike any outsider. They are the people God has placed in these communities to reach their neighbors with the gospel of Jesus Christ. *Do not overlook them on your mission trip.* Instead, make it a point to uplift them. To come alongside them in their ministries. To build them up, encourage them, and assist them. If you are truly going for maximum return on your investment, this is where you will find it. These local believers were in this community long before you arrived, and will be there long after you leave. Learn from them. Ask them in advance how your team can be utilized to assist them in their initiatives. Take time to pray over their pastor. Take their ministry leaders out for dinner. Invest in the leaders' spouses. Do everything you can to bless these people. This will go further than you will ever see.

I'm blessed to have the opportunity to develop relationships in new locations as a part of my work with a sending organization. I've assisted in developing new partnerships in locations from Alaska to Israel to the Dominican Republic. I've found that establishing genuine partnerships is easier in some locations than in others. A number of variables come into play, such as the local church's past missions organization experiences, cultural differences, and logistical challenges. In our organization, teams come from various churches across the U.S. for what's typically a week-long trip, with our goal being that they establish a long-term relationship with the congregation we partner them with. On a recent partnership development trip, I experienced an ideal scenario for local church-based missions. We're now in year two of having teams from our organization come for mission trips in this location, with the first year having met the typical bumps and trials. Now as our teams from the U.S. are returning to the same place for a second year, the local church leadership has begun to open up. They have gotten to know us better. Elements of trust are being established. They have experienced our teams, and seen the way these teams serve with the local congregations in their district.

On this recent trip, I was with our local staff, sitting in the living room of the pastor who oversees the district of local congregations in the area. We were talking about the successes and trials of year one. He was sharing his thoughts about the teams we'd sent, and how we could serve more effectively now in year two. This year we had a handful of teams returning to serve with the same partner congregation they served with last year (perfect!), and a handful of new teams that needed to be partnered. We shared with the pastor the overall skillsets of the new teams, and he worked to confirm dates with churches he felt would be a good fit to partner them with. That evening we had a dinner bringing together all the local pastors and their spouses who would be receiving teams. We answered questions, we prayed together, and we had discussions around true partnership. The pastors were eager to be able to utilize their assigned team as a tool for ministry in their community. The dreaming, scheming, and strategizing were flowing as the local pastors talked together about how they were going to use their teams. The lead pastor—the pastor of the pastors—gave his ideas and reflections about what he had seen happening already.

I sat there at that dinner, letting it sink in that what was happening in that time together is what God has placed on my heart for effective missions. I spent the weeks following this trip working with the teams from the U.S., talking to them about the hearts of their partner pastors and the ministries that their teams were being invited into. Dreaming and scheming with the teams on how to best use their gifts to uplift these local initiatives. Through this process, it's clear it isn't my, or our organization's, ministry that the team is entering into. This is the local church's ministry. I'm just a facilitator, a connecting point, and I love that.

It goes without saying that the local church is not perfect. Some local churches are tired and dying. Some leaders are all but burned out. Other churches seem to have it all together, but are dealing with trials unseen. Let's be real: There's no perfect church. Praise God that he recognizes that, and fills that gap through his son. Jesus is the fire that's burning in these churches. For some churches, that fire has been squelched, but even still, Jesus has not left. Will your team be the one to help fan the flame in those churches that are struggling? To offer encouragement, bringing life to a hurting and possibly dying congregation? What a privilege that would be. For other churches, the fire is raging with excitement and passion. What an opportunity it is to join in on that, to expand that ministry through the skillsets of your team.

The local church provides the framework for your team to have lasting impact. Will the log that any one team throws on the fire eventually burn up? Maybe. But will God add another one? Absolutely. The local church is the catalyst for reaching the world for Christ. The power within that is unstoppable.

> *And I tell you that you are Peter, and on this rock I will build my church, and the gates of [Hell] will not overcome it.*
> (Matthew 16:18)

Uniting the Global Church

The world is getting smaller. I could go from where I'm sitting right now to sitting across the table from a local pastor in Ghana within twenty-four hours. I can video chat any time with almost anyone I want—globally. Nearly 70 percent of the world's population has a cell phone, meaning I can talk to just about anyone I want—right now. Facebook, Twitter, WhatsApp, etc. all make it seamless to connect.

Google eliminates excuses for not having your facts straight about anything. People across the world are connecting, and in turn, people are making amazing strides in understanding each other. In the trade and business world, they call this globalization. Historically, there have been two major periods of advancement in globalization. The first was the result of colonization, and the second was the result of—you guessed it—technology. Global exports today are more than forty times greater than they were at the beginning of the twentieth century[1], meaning that the people around the world are depending on interconnectedness more than ever.

With the advancement of technology also comes the advancement of world travel. People are seeing the world like never before. Direct flights, app-based lodging (think VRBO and Airbnb), app-based transportation (Uber and Lyft), and endless online travel guides are making it easy to see places that twenty years ago you'd never even think of.

What does this mean for missions? It means that the church has more resources, more tools, and more ability to unite for the cause of Christ. It means that two congregations can have a real relationship from thousands of miles apart. It means resources, data, and effective strategies can be shared more quickly and easily than ever before.

Here's an example. One of the trends I've seen in recent years is an increase in the amount of international churches that are live streaming their services. Live streaming used to be reserved for a select group of mega churches. Now if I log into Facebook on a Sunday morning, I'll see a dozen-plus church services being broadcast live from congregations I've visited. What an opportunity this presents to gain a broader perspective. I can see God's people worshipping, in all their unique ways, from across the world. I've also seen how guest speakers have video conferenced in to share at churches from across the world. This was not possible twenty years ago.

Global church, it's time for us to roll. We have the opportunity to embrace technology as a tool for ministry and partnership—and I'm thankful to see that we are taking it.

I attribute the growth and health we have seen within the short-term missions movement to this awareness that has been brought by technology, as well as by previous failures. There's no doubt that countless missteps have taken place in missions. It's from these missteps, and a broadening perspective, that more effective and respectful short-term missions strategies have developed. I encourage ministry leaders not to live in the mistakes of the past. Yes, there have been many hurts caused in the name of missions. That said, don't throw the baby out with the bathwater. Don't succumb to the lie that it's impossible to make a positive impact in one week. Don't fall into the trap of believing that short-term missions are bad, and cause more harm than good. Those lies are simply that—lies.

With the advancement of technology, real long-distance relationships are possible. Utilize your short-term mission trip to enable that face-to-face contact with a partner congregation. Then continue that relationship through means that are now readily available. These "long-distance" relationships will no doubt broaden your church's global perspective, providing a taste of what heaven will look like as the global church comes together as one.

MY APPROACH

So how does one do short-term missions effectively in the context of local church partnerships? First, as I've noted previously, it is imperative that humility and respect are the guiding principles in any new partnership development. The primary goal is to build up and encourage local initiatives—not to impose your own. This is accomplished by intentionally listening, building trust, and adapting your personal preferences for the sake of local culture.

Let's address the goals of short-term missions as I see them. There are always exceptions to the goals, but when I consult with potential missions teams, our discussions are based on universal principles that I believe apply to all.

When I am asked what makes a successful mission trip, I often provide an answer similar to this:

There are three scenarios that I would call "success." In these scenarios, there's a "good," another "good," and then there's a "best" scenario.

- **Good:** The mission trip has a positive impact on your team, and a neutral impact on the community in which you are serving.
- **Good:** The mission trip has a neutral impact on your team, and a positive impact on the community.
- **Best:** The mission trip has a positive impact on both your team and the community.

The first scenario above introduces our first goal of short-term missions:

For each team member, the trip experience would broaden their perspective, and for some, change the trajectory of their life. If you gave me one week and asked that I take someone on an experience that would have the greatest potential to change their life, I'd take them on a mission trip. I've personally experienced the life-changing effect a mission trip can have. When an individual is immersed in a community that is not their own, there seems to be a veil lifted between them and their Creator. Oftentimes people are willing to take chances, doing things they normally wouldn't in the comforts of their home communities. Mission trips can serve as a discovery time for participants. I've seen many participants solidify their faith in Christ on their trips, and many others discover their passions and callings. **So the first goal is this: that the mission trip would have a life-changing, positive impact on your team.**

The second "good" scenario above introduces our second goal: that the mission trip would have a positive impact on the community in which you are serving. There are a lot of ways to measure this, many of them being not so good. For instance, if your team is serving in a community and providing $10,000 for a particular project, you could offend half the community and still be invited back. As I experienced in Haiti, the "yeses" sometimes flow a little too freely when you are the guest in another community. Many cultures are gifted in hospitality, and if you're not careful, your team can take advantage of this all too easily—and often unintentionally. I like to say that when your partner starts telling you no, that's when you know you are on the right track. So how do you measure whether you're having a positive impact on the local community? I believe this begins with establishing a healthy understanding of your team's place in the bigger picture. I'll write about this more extensively in the coming pages. The answer to this question is in many ways subjective, with the objectivity of it being realized as long-term relationships are established and testimonies begin to flow.

The "best" version of short-term missions is when the two goals come together. When the team members have a life-changing trip, and the local community is positively impacted. To create such an experience requires intentionality. I believe the life-changing experience for the team is the easy result to attain. It's having that collide with a positive impact on the community that can be challenging. Many sending organizations are structured to try to control this, with the organization working to take out as many variables as possible to ensure that this positive impact is achieved. Teams enter into programs where they'll take part in a replicable experience that can be perfected and refined as the following weeks of trips go on. Some of these organizations will work with local ministries and churches, and others will establish themselves as the local ministry, utilizing teams to uplift initiatives they have developed.

When I was a youth pastor prior to working full time in missions, I struggled to find an org that I felt operated in the sweet spot, one that would assist in facilitating our trips, but through which we'd be working with the local church. I wanted to serve in a community, but I didn't want to be the tenth team to serve that year in that community. I wanted a genuine partnership because of my deep belief in the power of the local church. I was looking for the best version of short-term missions, which makes a lasting impact on your team while leaving the local church encouraged and uplifted as they continue to serve their communities long after your team is gone.

Every week as part of my job, I speak to potential missions group leaders, giving my pitch for local church-based missions and why I believe they are effective. I can almost see the light bulb go on during those conversations as I speak the words that many people already have in their hearts. Sometimes I'm self-conscious because it's almost too simple:

"Once you have identified your team's skillsets and giftings, we will partner you with a local church where you can use those same skillsets to assist existing ministries."

"My goal is to see you develop a real, long-term relationship with a local congregation where you can return year after year."

"We work to only partner one or two teams with a church each year because the goal is to assist their ministry, not take over their ministry."

"You will stay right in the community, living and serving alongside the local church."

"All the ministry your team will do is directed by, and under the authority of, local leadership."

I then hear the stories and questions:

"Last year our team was split up and we built four houses."

"How many people fit at the missions base?"

"Do we need to pack our food? Last year they gave us a list of what to bring in our suitcases."

So although this chapter is meant to be philosophical, the practical elements are so closely intertwined that it's important to lay them out.

So, here's the practical side of making a community-based, church partnership trip happen:

Finding a Church Partner

Finding a church partner to invest in and assist while you are on missions can have its challenges. It is important that the church you are partnering with has leadership with integrity, and is not simply giving you empty yeses. They should truly desire to receive your team well and utilize your team to advance ongoing ministries.

For each new location that I am involved in developing—in other words, helping to partner U.S. teams with congregations around the world—the first objective is to identify the broader church leadership in that location. These people have been put in leadership by their peers (and God!), and as a result, connecting with them is the most healthy place to start. It is important that as we establish partner churches within a location where we will send teams, we are doing so under the direction and authority of these overarching leaders. If done well and with respect, these leaders often become our biggest advocates. When planning for upcoming missions, we present these leaders with information about the U.S. teams we anticipate joining us that year. Those leaders then place each team with the most appropriate church based on the giftings of each team and the needs of the local churches in the area.

From there, I and those I work with meet with the local churches and establish the connection between them and the sending missions team. I am confident in these partnerships because they were identified by leaders within the broader church.

Do not rely on Google, Facebook, or a friend's recommendation to find a partner church. It is imperative that we work through local church leadership and rely on their wisdom when it comes to understanding the broader context and creating partnerships. This is one key of doing partner-based, local church missions well, and it is missed by many.

Unity on Missions

There's a mistaken belief in our culture that if we're not living life adamantly *against* something, or adamantly *for* something, then we don't care about that something at all. We begin to surround ourselves with people who share our views, and consider others the enemies—or at least treat them like we do. This is very evident within church culture. Theological views have divided the church for centuries, resulting in hundreds of Christian denominations being established within the United States alone. Communities are dotted with half-empty church buildings on every corner, representing the various denominations in that region. Thankfully, through technology and other means, I believe we're starting to see a shift within the younger generations of the church. We're seeing more and more churches coordinating events with each other, sharing buildings, and joining in ministry together. I'm hopeful that this shift toward unity is only just beginning.

I believe there is a place for denominations, different theological perspectives, and all of that. It's healthy and good to continue to refine our relationship with our Savior. But when on missions and in life, there's only one qualifier for whether we can partner together. Here it is:

Do you believe Jesus died on the cross, was buried, and rose again on the third day? Do you believe that through his death and resurrection alone your sins are forgiven for all eternity?

If the answer is yes, then let's go. Let's lay down our differences for the sake of the gospel, focusing on what unites us and not what divides us. This is what I encourage, and require, the teams I work with to do. This is what we encourage the local churches we partner with to do.

There's freedom in recognizing that you disagree with someone, but for the purposes of the cross, for this week of missions, it doesn't matter. Take a deep breath—and serve. It's beautiful. Baptists, Presbyterians, Covenants, Methodists, Lutherans, Protestants, Catholics—do you believe in the salvation of Jesus Christ? If yes, then we're ready to go. We've got work to do.

I bring this up in the context of this book for a few reasons. The church association your congregation is a part of may require that you work with someone within your denomination when you travel for missions. And even if this isn't the case, you will at minimum have people within your congregation, or your team, who will be vocal in their belief that you should not serve with a church that has different theological views than yours does. I'd encourage you to be prepared for this, and to push back respectfully. I can tell you this from my personal testimony: Breaking down the walls of denominations in the context of missions is a beautiful thing. The other reason I tell you this is that denominations tend to be very regional. If you are set on serving a church within a particular denomination, you will likely eliminate large regions of the world from potential partnerships. For instance, years ago when I had the opportunity to lead teams to Jamaica, there was only one Lutheran church on the entire island. If the Lutheran teams coming to Jamaica required that they only work with Lutherans, that one church would soon have been overrun with missions groups, and other churches may have had no partners at all.

If you are avoiding missions that involve church partnership due to theological reasons, take a step back and reevaluate your priorities as a Jesus follower and a member of his church.

Under Authority

After you have been matched with a church partner, you should plan your week hand-in-hand with local leadership. As you are planning your mission trip, the local church should have veto power over anything you put on the schedule. This isn't intended to squelch your input into what the week will look like, but instead provides an avenue for you to maximize your team's efforts to uplift real ministry. As you are planning your trip, it is important for church leadership to know your team's skillsets and interests, and then for the local church to inform you of the best way to use your team in the context of their ministry. It's important to flesh out the skill levels and maturity of your team as well. Be realistic and honest, as this conversation will shape expectations the host church will have for your team. If your team is young and new to missions, share that. If your team has veteran ministry leaders and skilled workers, share that. And guess what: While you are serving, if the local church wants to change the schedule, you should let them. Be in constant communication with the local church leadership, molding and shaping the trip based on how the Spirit leads and the logistics fall.

This is also the place to consider cultural sensitivity. Communicate with your host partner and research the local culture carefully. Your team will be immersed in this community. It is imperative that your team be respectful of local customs. This includes dressing appropriately and recognizing that your team will be viewed as outsiders and as such, your actions and words will come under a microscope. You'll find that in many situations locals will overlook minor things, but that will not change the fact that creating distractions in ministry reduces your effectiveness. Your team should recognize that your actions are reflected on the local church, and more specifically, the local pastor. If something goes wrong, that pastor is often on the hook. The moral of this story is to have an intentional conversation with both your host and team prior to the trip. If you do this, you'll be in good shape.

Use Your Natural Tendencies

Your team members have many skillsets and ministry giftings. Your team is a small representation of the body of Christ, with each individual gifted in their own unique and specific way. As a whole, you might have universal skillsets, such as a stellar children's ministry team or a particularly handy construction group. Or you might have a youth group made up of individuals who don't yet know their skillsets but want to serve. Whatever the makeup of your group, my suggestion is this: Avoid the canned experiences. In other words, avoid experiences where your team's uniqueness is overlooked. Where team after team engages in the same exact activities, week after week. Where your all-star kids ministry team is stuck building a house each day of their trip. It's possible to have stories of changed lives in such experiences, mine being one of them with my Vancouver trip during my teenage years, but we are going for maximum return on investment here. We're looking to plug your team into a big picture: a global-church-minded, world-reaching picture in which we're united for Christ.

Utilize your team's specific skills and giftings to encourage, build up, and assist the local church. Analyze your team. Spend time working with them to hear their hearts and interests. I'd suggest working through personality or spiritual gift tests with your group. Once you are able to identify the natural tendencies, giftings, and interests of your team, you will have a much easier time partnering your team with an appropriate church and designing a missions experience that will have maximum impact.

Return to the Same Community Year after Year

A pastor I know who oversees multiple churches tells our teams this all the time: "If you come once, it's good. If you come twice, it's better." What he is articulating is the value of long-term relationships. Where I have seen this be most effective is when churches have a unique partnership that is not clouded by dozens of missions teams on a yearly basis. It's important that if a host church is receiving missions teams, those missions teams are building up the local church's ministry, not taking over their ministry. I've seen churches receive ten or more teams a year, and the reputation that they begin to develop in the community as the "missions team" church.

I would encourage you to develop a unique relationship with a local church, and then return year after year. If the church you are working with is also receiving teams from multiple other churches, then know that this might hinder a genuine partnership from developing. Use discernment, and remember that you are going for maximum return on investment. Choose a partner and sending organization that can ensure your time and financial investment is being utilized to uplift lasting, local initiatives.

I've had the opportunity to lead multiple teams back to their partnership church for repeat trips. This is without a doubt one of the most impactful elements of church-based global missions. When I first introduce a sending group leader to a local host pastor, there's an excitement in the air, and a sense of gratefulness to serve together. But the really good stuff is after the trip, when I debrief with the group leader and they tell me that they desire to return. That's when I get to call the host pastor, debrief with them, and then share with them the desire of the team to enter into a long-term relationship. This is gold, and something that you can't replicate with any other missions model. To see two congregations from two different cultures encouraging and building into each other. To be able to lead teams as they serve in the same community for the seventh, eighth, or ninth year in a row. To see partnership infiltrate both congregations so that it's not just a U.S.-based ministry going or a host pastor benefiting, but two churches partnering. These scenarios are not only possible, but I see them time and time again. You can do this—it's the twenty-first century.

FINAL THOUGHTS

So how did I mess it up on the side of the mountain back in 2010? The trips I lead typically start with travel on Saturday. This is intentional because the trip essentially launches on Sunday morning with a church worship service. This is an incredible way to start the week, worshiping with your partnering church and sharing time together in God's word. Sunday afternoons are typically relational, where teams will play with kids, do home visits, host adult Bible studies, etc. If a team indicates prior to the trip that they would like to be involved in service projects, we'll typically begin these on Monday. I'm always preaching to teams that projects are just a means to show that you care in a different way. The reality is the local people around you could probably do the task a lot quicker, and likely a lot better, than most missions teams can. Teams are often used to do the grunt work, hiring local workers to do the skilled labor. In the end, it's not about the work you get done, but the relationships you build along the way.

Well, on that 2010 trip, I had forgotten (or hadn't yet learned) some of those core principles. A couple hours into our service project, I saw our team members sitting around, interacting with some of the locals. On the schedule it was construction time, and I was concerned that I wasn't doing my job by facilitating the ministries we had planned. I looked around to see what I could get our team involved in, and proceeded to try to set an example. I walked over to where the locals were mixing cement and lifted an 80lb sack of dry mix to add to the pile. I heaved the sack from my shoulder onto the previously dumped-out bags. If you've worked with cement before, you know that its dry form has the consistency of powdered sugar. POOF. A cloud of dry mix filled the air. I looked up, an "Ooops" rolling off my lips, to see three local workers as white as snow, dry mix sticking to their sweat-drenched skin. The stare-down they gave sticks (pun intended) with me to this day. The rest of my team was happily interacting with local people, while I had a group of workers angry at me. "Man, that was stupid," I uttered as I sheepishly walked away. I was right with those words, and so wrong with my previous actions. What the team was doing was what Jesus would have been doing— focusing on people, not projects or the itinerary. In that moment, I was grateful for grace.

If you're thinking about planning a short-term mission trip with a group, know this: God has called you and equipped you to do this well. God designed his people, his church, to be one with each other. To partner together. This includes people from different cultures. Act justly, love mercy, walk humbly. This is what the Lord has called you to. If you have a posture that truly models this, you can be confident that there is incredible power in utilizing your team to develop a partnership with a cross-cultural church. The world is connecting like never before. Church, this is our time to unite and do the same.

RESPONSE

JON HUCKINS

I loved reading and learning from Jim Noreen's life and experience in short-term missions. As I read this chapter, it felt like I was reading Jim's heart as reflected in some of his deepest convictions. There was a lot I resonated with, as well as a few things that raised questions and concerns. I'll start with the stuff that resonated.

Jim's posture of humility and ongoing learning was not only reflected in his philosophy of missions, but his writing. Humility isn't everything, but it's a big deal. I'm more convinced than ever that the church needs fewer strong and powerful leaders and more humble and tender ones. This is especially true when it comes to international missions, where white Christians from the West have often entered into other countries in the posture of colonizers rather than collaborators. Additionally, Jim's emphasis on the need for churches to work with other churches is right on. These kinds of partnerships, if done well, lead to mutual learning, deepened trust, and a cultural competency that is necessary for long-term relationships. Finally, I really appreciated Jim's call to transcend denominational and doctrinal boundaries, instead focusing on a common commitment to Jesus. It's that kind of expansive faith that creates room for big impact.

As for questions and concerns, here we go:

First, is it possible to build equitable relationships with churches if the relationship always requires that the dominant culture Christians *come* to and do work *for* the non-dominant-culture churches? No matter the intention or spirit of collaboration with local leaders, there is a power dynamic that has to be acknowledged and intentionally addressed if there is to be mutual relationship. Some call this equity. What if as much energy and resources were given to learning *from* the Indigenous leaders—in the form of culture immersion, pre-trip study, etc.—as were used for bringing a good or service to them? What if we raised an equal amount of money to fund Indigenous leaders

to come to our churches in the U.S. as part of a binational learning experience?

Second, requiring a local church to be involved in short-term missions makes a lot of sense—but is concerning in two ways:

- I know for a fact that Indigenous pastors representing their communities to outside missions organizations can be put in impossible situations. They sometimes become the "yes" men (because it's usually men) of the missions organization because of the power dynamic I bring up in my previous point, or they can be very antagonistic to the local community they serve. In my organization, we have worked in many communities where the local pastor became the primary access point to international aid/money/support, creating a dynamic of competition and resentment among locals. The local pastors then have power over the local community and can play favorites with where they point the support. This can destabilize entire communities.

- Only working with churches cuts out relationships and collaboration with those outside the church context who are doing equally beautiful work. While functionally convenient, working with churches can blind us to the gift of those doing kingdom work equal to (and, at times, much better than) that of those inside its constructs. My experience has been that partnerships with those doing kingdom work outside the church not only expand our collective worldview, but allow us to see ourselves as part of a much bigger mission God is weaving into our world.

Finally, the long-term formation of participants requires an intentionality that extends far beyond a one-off experience. In Jim's model, participants will be impacted, their worldviews will expand, and there is no doubt change will occur. But, without intentionally focusing on what they are being formed into, I'm concerned it will be difficult to sustain. We can still hide in the renovation of a church building without confronting the stuff that needs to be renovated in us. My team often says, "The mission begins when we land back home." What formational footholds are being offered that translate a powerful experience into a renewed way of life?

All that said, this was a blast and I'm thrilled to learn of so many thoughtful ways people are seeking to be living reflections of good news in our world. Let's keep at it together!

VIEW 3:
APPROACHING URBAN MISSIONS AS LIFE-LONG LEARNERS, ADVOCATES, AND ALLIES

BY SUSIE GAMEZ

INTRODUCTION

I didn't grow up in urban America. In fact, I wasn't even raised in the U.S. So who am I and why am I writing about this? I like to describe myself as being Korean by heritage, Canadian by birth, Mexican by marriage, and American by immigration. Fresh out of college at twenty-two, I relocated from a middle-class suburban neighborhood in Vancouver, Canada, to South Central Los Angeles. I was a missionary with an urban church planting organization. Though I knew very little about the world of church planting, I felt called to serve the urban poor in LA, but I also felt called to serve the larger church. This organization felt like the perfect fit because it did both. Young and inexperienced, I was willing and ready to learn on the job. My initial commitment to serve with this organization was for one to three years, but I ended up staying for fourteen. For many of those years, I was also slowly but surely working on my Master's in Intercultural Studies at Fuller Theological Seminary. Thousands of dollars and many seminary papers later, I realized that my greatest education was being absorbed and experienced out on the streets and in the homes of my neighbors. The people I learned from and the neighborhood I lived in created a community that I loved deeply and an endearing place that I called home.

During my time in South Central, my ministry was primarily with youth and young adults. When it came to missions groups, I spent a lot of time hosting other youth groups. They all came with good hearts and the intention to serve the poor, do good works, and share the good news. But when I would get to talking to the leaders of these groups about the objectives of their trips, their main focus seemed to be exposing their youth to a world outside of their own bubble and creating opportunities for them to serve the less fortunate. A great majority of these groups were made up of white upper-class or middle-class teens from places very different from South Central LA. From these leaders, I would often hear lament about how sheltered their youth were and hopes that this trip would help the youth not take for granted all of the things they had been "blessed" with. If you already sense where I'm going with this, I'm sure you can feel my tinge of disdain here.

Before I go there, I'll say this. I get it. Like I said, the *intentions* of these short-term missions groups were good and not entirely wrong. My husband is employed by an organization that works to help alleviate poverty in some of the poorest countries in the world. We live in the tension of the poverty we see in the two thirds world and the wealth we live with here in America. We have four young kids, and from time to time we also fall into the same trap, perpetuating the myth that having more materially means we are also more blessed spiritually. While our kids should absolutely be thankful that they never have to worry about where their next meal will come from or where they will be sleeping day to day, the implicit message we send when we tell our kids and youth to remember those who are "less fortunate" is that we are more blessed and therefore favored by God because of all that we have. This is dangerous thinking that can lead the non-poor to have god complexes and savior mentalities.

MY PRIORITIES

Important Things to Talk About First

Jackie Hill Perry, a writer, speaker, and artist, once wrote on social media, "Why aren't there mission trips to rich suburban neighborhoods? Because those Christians mistakenly believe that impoverished = unrighteous."[1]

If your understanding of the "inner city" is informed through the lens of mainstream media, it might not be hard to understand why poverty seems to be synonymous with a lack of righteousness. The never-ending news cycles that report on the violence, drugs, theft, and general deviancy that occur in low-income communities make it hard for anyone to see all the beauty, goodness, and wisdom that are abundant in urban communities like South Central Los Angeles.

What makes the conversation about inner city America a little confusing is the changing nature of the "inner city" or "urban America" today. Two decades ago, one could reference a city in urban America and a stereotypical (but not completely inaccurate) snapshot would appear, one of a densely populated, low-income, non-white, primarily black or Latino neighborhood. There was a much clearer dichotomy between urban/suburban, rich/poor, and black/white twenty years ago than there is now. Gentrification and changing immigration patterns along with other factors have caused a shift in the landscape and culture of urban America. For the sake of clarity (though this is admittedly archaic), I will reference "urban America" as urban city communities that largely remain stratified by race, income, and overall social class.

Books like *Toxic Charity* by Robert Lupton and *When Helping Hurts* by Steve Corbett and Brian Fikkert have given us a glimpse into how some of our best intentions can in fact hurt communities more than they are helping. In this chapter, I will be discussing short-term missions from an urban perspective—pointing out some ways that STMs have negatively impacted urban communities and suggesting ways that they can be done better. Before getting to that, however, it is important to dig in to a bit of a historical framework for understanding. To do so, in the first half of this chapter we'll touch upon the inextricable ties between racism and poverty in America.

Poverty and Race
Passed down through many generations, the ideology of the

protestant work ethic has widely contributed to the thinking that being materially prosperous or financially successful is the result of hard work and personal merit. To put it plainly, in many people's minds poor equals bad—or stupid, lazy, shameful, worthy of blame, and the result of bad choices. Rich equals good, smart, diligent, praiseworthy, and the fruit of good choices. While it is not untrue that hard work and good stewardship can lead to financial success, it's also true that reducing financial prosperity to the result of work ethic and other virtuous attributes is misleading and harmful, particularly for people of color.

I say this because historically, the majority of wealthy people in America have been white. In a rapidly diversifying and seemingly less segregated America, many people believe that the wealth gap is narrowing, but in reality economic disparity between racial groups is actually growing. According to a 2018 article in *Forbes* magazine, by 2020 the median white household will own 86 times more wealth than its black counterpart, and 68 times more wealth than its Latino counterpart. That same article cites the *New York Times*, which states that for every $100 in white family wealth, black families possess just $5.04.[2] That gap is too wide for comfort and ought to be deemed unacceptable to all of us.

If you feel an objection rising up in you, I will quickly address a point here. Yes, there are many poor white people in America. In fact, according to the National Center for Children in Poverty, white children make up the largest number of America's poor. But while numerically there are indeed more white children in poverty, a much higher *percentage* of non-white children in America are poor. According to national averages from 2018 (in some states the margins are much higher), 33 percent of black children are living in poverty and 27 percent of Latino children are living in poverty. Meanwhile 12 percent of Asian children and 10 percent of white children live in poverty. Finally, though they do not make up a large percentage of the overall population, it is worth noting that a heartbreaking 40 percent of Native American children live in poverty—in one of the wealthiest and arguably the most powerful nation in the world.[3]

Why are there such disparities in wealth among the different racial/ethnic groups in America? In short it's because, as Cornel West famously penned years ago, "race matters."[4] "White privilege" has become a controversial (and triggering) phrase for many people. Some will argue that the entire premise of white privilege is a myth and others will say that the term is unfairly used and needlessly divisive. In the interest of staying faithful to the topic at hand I won't dive too deep into a debate about that here. But the existence of white privilege does not mean that white people do not experience poverty, and neither does it mean that white people do not suffer or experience injustice. While white privilege is not solely economic in its function, it is willfully ignorant to discount the numerous advantages white people in America have had over people of color when it comes to opportunity for financial success and overall well-being.

The poverty we see in "urban America" is not the result of entire people groups making bad decisions, refusing to work hard, or being inherently bad, stupid, and lazy (I hope reading that sentence felt as ludicrous to read as it felt for me to write). But while it is easy for people to see the audaciousness of a statement like that, it is not as easy for people to admit that America remains systemically racist and unjust at its core.

Generational wealth (or at least access to wealth) is a benefit that cannot be underestimated and is key to understanding the dynamics of urban poverty today. All the way back to the genocide and oppression of the Indigenous peoples and their land, American history is rife with shameful practices that gave white people an unfair advantage over all other groups.

Poverty, Race, and the Church

The "founding fathers" of this nation grossly misused and misinterpreted Scripture as a means to justify their sin. Meanwhile, the mainstream evangelical church has not done an adequate job of confessing and lamenting over the sins of our nation. I would assert that because of this inadequacy, repentance for sins of the past has also been incomplete. From today's perspective, some sins seem obvious to most of us—like the enslavement of millions of African men and women, racist and unjust labor laws, discriminatory immigration and voting laws, and segregation. Though less obviously problematic to some, one would hope that the church would also be more vocal about current injustices like under-resourced schools (particularly in areas densely populated by black and Latino populations),[5] unequal pay,[6] unequal access to health care, racial profiling, police brutality, and mass incarceration under a system that disproportionately penalizes people of color, and with more severity.[7] Instead, we find ourselves having to fight to prove that these experiences and inequalities are real and not imagined.

Systemic racism and injustice has negatively impacted entire communities of color throughout American history. Unfortunately it seems to take decades for the blinders to come off, making hindsight much clearer than the present vision. The legacy of Dr. Martin Luther King Jr. is evidence of this kind of slow buffering.

In the months and years leading up to his assassination, Dr. King was considered a troublemaker and rebel-rouser by white evangelicals. Dr. King's exhortations to the church to take up the fight against injustice were met with opposition and defensiveness. He was accused of focusing too much on "social issues" rather than "spiritual" ones (does this sound familiar?).[8] Now hailed as a hero for the masses, his words are selectively quoted in sermons and celebrated nationally. It seems that Dr. King's activism and prophetic voice have been sanitized and the mainstream church's opposition to his message has been downplayed—even forgotten. Remember that thing about America not being good at confessing, lamenting, and repenting of its past sins? Much of the white evangelical church was guilty by omission during the civil rights era. We celebrate the actions of a few, but forget to lament and learn from the inaction and lack of courage of the many.

In an article for *The Washington Post*, Jemar Tisby (president of The Witness: A Black Christian Collective) writes about why so many white churches resisted Dr. King's call to action. Tisby recalls Dr. King's speech "I Have Seen the Mountaintop" and he quotes this excerpt:

> *"It's all right to talk about long white robes over yonder, in all of its symbolism,"* he said, *"but ultimately people want some suits and dresses and shoes to wear down here. It's all right to talk about streets flowing with milk and honey, but God has commanded us to be concerned about the slums down here and His children who can't eat three square meals a day."*
>
> *"It's all right to talk about the new Jerusalem, but one day God's preacher must talk about the new New York, the new Atlanta, the new Philadelphia, the new Los Angeles, the new Memphis, Tennessee."*[9]

Dr. King wrote this during a time when perhaps it was more difficult to get people to see why feeding the poor and assisting the needy were essential parts of proclaiming the good news. In this day and age I don't think it would be hard to rally volunteers to serve in soup kitchens and donate clothes—but a "new Los Angeles" or a "new Philadelphia" in a way that really answers the prayer "Thy Kingdom come, Thy will be done on earth as it is in Heaven" goes much deeper than superficial fixes that don't have a lasting impact.

Word and Deed

One might say that whatever we do here on earth doesn't matter if it doesn't point us toward and prepare us for eternity. This is true. Scriptures like Colossians 3:2, which admonishes readers to "set your minds on things above, not on earthly things," and Matthew 6, which encourages us to store up our treasures in heaven rather than here on earth, are good examples of why we should focus our efforts on eternity.

But let us remember that Jeremiah was instructed to seek the shalom (meaning peace, wholeness, presence of the Lord) of the city in Jeremiah 29:7. Another verse that has found a resurgence in its popularity and importance in the last couple of decades is Micah 6:8. This Scripture not only instructs us to love mercy and walk humbly with our God, but it exhorts us to *act* justly. Faith without works is dead, as it says in James 2, and Ephesians 2:10 tells us that we are God's handiwork, created in Christ Jesus to *do* good works. Though the list could go on, Hebrews 10:24-25 seems to bring together the idea of setting our minds on things above and living out our faith and good works in the here and now:

> *And let us consider how we may spur one another on toward love and good deeds, not giving up meeting together, as some are in the habit of doing, but encouraging one another—and all the more as you see the Day approaching.*

As the day approaches—with eternity in mind—let us love and do good works. This seems to correct the cliché, "don't be so heavenly-minded that you are no earthly good." Because of Hebrews 10:25, one might reimagine that saying with new wording: "Be *so* heavenly-minded that you will be determined to do the utmost *earthly* good." That way, whether we eat or drink, everything we do will be done unto the glory of God (1 Corinthians 10:31).

There are so many more Scriptures that can point us to the importance of our faith being lived out in both word and deed, proclamation and demonstration, and in nurturing the well-being of people to be both whole and holy…but I think you get the point. God cares for all people while they are here on earth and for eternity. If we are in Christ Jesus we can offer the goodness of his kingdom wherever we go.

In light of all that was written above about poverty not being equal to unrighteousness and material wealth not being equal to God's favor and blessing, what then does it look like to be on mission with God without fostering a god complex in the non-poor? STMs certainly have a place in fulfilling the Great Commission and can be good expressions of loving our neighbors. But beyond poverty alleviation efforts, there must be a fight against injustice and a genuine partnership in bringing "kingdom shalom" to cities.

As Jesus was the fulfillment of Isaiah's prophecy, we must continue to be the fulfillment of the ministry Jesus began:

"The Spirit of the Lord is on me,
  because he has anointed me
  to proclaim good news to the poor.
He has sent me to proclaim freedom for the prisoners
  and recovery of sight for the blind,
to set the oppressed free,
  to proclaim the year of the Lord's favor."

(Luke 4:18-19)

MY APPROACH

Doing Good... but Better

Switching gears, I will now give practical suggestions on how short-term mission trips in urban communities can be done better. Beneath my suggestions, I have included some examples of what not to do and stories that exemplify why sometimes well-intended efforts have hurt more than they've helped.

BE A GOOD STUDENT
Before You Go, Study the History of the Community

Ask a lot of questions and be curious about the community you hope to serve. How have things changed over the past few decades? Why have they changed and how has that affected the community? A quick Google search can actually be quite helpful for some background knowledge.

When I lived in South Central LA, my neighborhood had many characteristics typical of an "inner city" neighborhood. Amidst all of the beauty and richness that I love to highlight, it's hard to ignore the reality that gang violence was prevalent, drugs were rampant, poverty was apparent, and dysfunctional families were not hard to find. These were the things that made South Central LA a "less desirable" community to many. It wasn't always this way, though. At one point, the West Adams district was one of the wealthiest neighborhoods in Los Angeles. It was a wealthy white community until the early 1910s when West LA, Hollywood, and Beverly Hills were being developed. As white people started to migrate to those areas, those from the wealthy black community started moving in. Notable celebrities like Ray Charles, Joe Louis, and Little Richard all owned homes in the area. This is when "white flight" really took off, and eventually the area became a primarily African-American community, and now more than 56 percent of the population is Latino (followed by African-American).[10]

In my particular community it was also important to know the geography and history of gangs. MS-13 is one of the largest and most notorious gangs in the world. Started in El Salvador, MS-13 also became prominent in our neighborhood, causing more factions and violence along with it. The Rollin' 20s were Bloods, and the Rollin' 30s were Crips. 20th Street down to 29th was territory marked by Bloods, and as soon as you crossed over to the 30s you were in Crip territory. Bloods and Crips have been at odds with one another for years. Add in other subset gangs like 18th Street, and in a half-mile radius you have several gangs at war with one another.[11]

There are other questions that would be useful to ask when traveling to an urban community for any STM, ones that would best be answered by those living and working in the community. Like, who are the stakeholders in the community? What are some of the most pervasive problems? What are some of the most promising prospects? And perhaps most fundamentally, how can you pray? These are just a few examples of potential questions.

Be Intentional in Learning About the Culture

Engaging in short-term missions within the U.S. does not mean that you will not be engaging with people cross-culturally, so find out who lives there. What ethnic groups are prominent in the community you will visit, and what are some key things you should learn about the culture and about cross-cultural engagement?

There are over 4.5 billion Asian people in the world. Not all Asian people are Chinese. Likewise, not all Latino people are Mexican, and not all black people are African-American. Many people assume that South Central LA is culturally African-American and Mexican. The street I lived on, however, had a good number of black people who

were Belizean and did not identify as "African-American." The area
I lived in also had a great number of immigrants from El Salvador.
Much to their chagrin, immigrants from Guatemala, Honduras, and
Nicaragua often tend to get lumped in as "Mexican." Depending on
where you are and who you ask, some of these groups might also be
at odds with one another, so it is important to know these distinctions
when interacting with people. The simple act of taking interest in
people's cultures and countries of origin can be very endearing. Not
doing so can be polarizing and divisive, furthering the cultural divide.

As noted above, knowing gang territories and history is important
and it is useful in cultural engagement. The block I lived on was near
the dividing line between two gangs. When we would host Bible
Clubs in our yard, kids from just a few streets over would want to
come but refuse when invited because of where we were located.
Whether because of a perceived danger in being in rival gang
territory or because of a genuine allegiance to their block, divisions
like these can start as early as infancy and can be deeply embedded.
While the goal of unification is lofty, perhaps your group members
should be prepared to multiply their efforts and offer outreach events
in more than one location.

Ask Your Hosts for Their Expertise
Don't go with your own agenda. Ask your host how you may be most
useful and effective.

Our missions organization hosted many types of groups. While
over time we did make a greater attempt to streamline our efforts
and create better boundaries on what we could and could not do
when hosting groups, most of these visiting groups were "financial
partners" to our ministry. This meant that there was often a great
degree of accommodating *their needs.* Some groups would come
with preconceived notions about what they would like to do and how
they'd like to do it. Some might have prepared a Vacation Bible School
curriculum they'd had great success with in their own community,
and they would come wanting to replicate the experience for the
kids in our community. There was often no thought to cross-cultural
relevance for the kids and most of the time there was no "culture

training" given to their volunteers before they came.

Clean-up projects, painting walls, and building projects, capped off with a community hamburger/hot dog BBQ, also seemed to be part of the standard menu for most groups. Cost-effectiveness may be the motivating factor here, but to really speak the culturally relevant "heart language" of the people when it comes to food, a BBQ/cookout would be really inviting if the menu involved *carne asada* and *elote* or BBQ ribs and hot links.

Missions organizations must get better at articulating these types of concerns and do a better job of preparing the groups they host. The sad reality is that for many organizations, bending over backward for financial partners is an accepted norm that has yet to find its way out of the system.

Remember That You Are Not the Hero
Jesus is the Savior. You are not. Repeat.

Bryant Myers, former VP of World Vision and author of *Walking with the Poor*, identifies a dichotomy between the poor and the non-poor. He says the wealthy often suffer from god complexes and the poor suffer from marred identity. Each of these identities is rooted in brokenness and neither of these identities is a picture of the wholeness that God intends for us.[12]

Humility must be the starting point for anyone who wants to go serve anywhere or anyone. Not only did Jesus already come to "save the hood," the people of the culture you represent may have actually done a lot more harm than good in that community, so make no room for your ego to go with you. As stated at length above, there is a history of racism and oppression in America that we should not ignore. The god complexes of the wealthy become further embedded when we approach STMs with the idea that the non-poor have more to offer than the poor, and that God's favor rests on the wealthy.

Gideon Yung asked this question: "Why are rich countries the ones sending short-term missionaries? Are Christians from rich countries more gifted than those from poor countries?"[13] The answer is obviously no, but read the beatitudes (or really, all of the Scriptures about Jesus's ministry) if you have any doubt about this. The same question can be asked about the poor and the non-poor here in America, and it points back to the very similar question posed by Jackie Hill Perry at the beginning of this chapter. The bottom line is simply that it costs money to be "sent," and funds to support STMs are more quickly and readily available to the rich.

A well-known saying amongst preachers and evangelists is that "we are all just beggars telling other hungry people where to find bread." That may be true in theory, but it just doesn't seem to play out that way when it comes to dictating who goes on STMs here in the U.S.

One idea to remedy this reality and help foster greater missions efforts from among the poor is to create a partnership where wealthier churches can allocate a tithe or offering toward mobilizing missions for the poor. Not *to* the poor, but *for* the financially under-resourced to be able to mobilize for missions themselves. Perhaps your church could even do a dollar-for-dollar match, where every dollar raised for STMs within your own church would be matched with a dollar given to a missionary from a less financially-endowed church.

Finally, let us also be reminded that more often than not, God is already at work in the communities STMs go to. Think about how many times you have heard people say, "I think I got more out of it than they did" upon returning from a mission trip. You could probably say this rings true for yourself as well. I often tell people that ironically, in my time as a missionary, I learned how to love God and love my neighbor through the example set by those I went to "serve." There is a level of love and concern for one another that the poor can model so beautifully to all of us, but if we do not have a posture of humility or a desire to learn from other as bearers of the imago Dei, we will miss it.

Go as a Learner
Your culture is not the standard.

To put it bluntly, here in America there has been a deeply embedded lie that "the white way is the right way." The values of the mainstream white majority have forced all of us to assimilate to some degree. For one to do well in school, one must adopt the ways of the white majority. To get a job and keep that job, let alone hope for advancements and promotions, one must follow the rules laid down and kept by the white majority. Efficiency, timeliness, direct and to-the-point communication styles, low-power distance, and individualistic thinking are all characteristics of mainstream American values.

Many people in the communities you will go to serve (and learn from) do not function according to those same rules. They will most likely be more event-oriented than time-oriented, people-oriented over task-oriented, and collectivist rather than individualistic. This will mean that parties or events that are said to start at 3:00 p.m. might not really start until about 5:00 and no one will be mad about it. The invitation might have said the party is supposed to end at 7:00, but it will probably go well past 9:00. Letting events happen around the activity of the people is more important than sticking to a schedule, and connecting with people is more important than accomplishing a task. Collectivist communities think as groups and focus on how individual actions affect the whole group, rather than viewing themselves as separate people whose actions have no reflection on their entire community.

There is much to be learned from one another's cultures. It is difficult to say if one way is right or wrong, better or worse. The thing to remember is that every culture bears a reflection of the image of God, and kingdom culture is inclusive and diverse. When the images of Revelation 7 come to pass and the great multitude from every tribe, tongue, and nation cry out before the Lamb, no one language or culture will dominate over another. We will all be submitted to the King and he will bring all things together in perfect unity.

Acknowledge and Celebrate the Imago Dei in Everyone
Do your part to help restore dignity to others.

One highlight for our youth was yearly summer camp. The organization I worked with owned a campsite up in the mountains two hours north of the city. One year, a "short-term missionary" (a summer intern at the camp) stood before hundreds of teens and shared his testimony. In his story, he talked about a mission trip he'd gone on with his church the summer before, speaking at length about the poverty he saw in Haiti. He said he was shocked at how dirty, poor, and dangerous the country was. Being the only white people in the area, the presence of his group was very noticeable and he said they were literally "risking their lives" being there. He went on to talk about all the things God taught him that summer about faith, courage, and selfless service. His only references to Haiti were about how bad, scary, and impoverished it was.

We had a few Haitian students with us that summer. One girl broke down in tears during cabin time, hurt and angry about how she was made to feel dirty, poor, and dangerous. Her mother had sent her, along with her older brother, to the U.S. to flee a dangerous situation, but despite that, Haiti was still "home," and loving, courageous, and strong people like her mother were part of what made Haiti beautiful. Thankfully there were sisters there to remind her that loving, courageous, and strong Haitians like her mother, and loving, courageous, and strong Haitians like herself, carry the imago Dei (image of God).

Don't Do for People What They Can Do for Themselves

Before you start a project, ask the question, "Are we doing something that a person from this community could be doing instead?" Your good intentions may be taking business away from locals. Look for ways to foster partnership and development within the community. Building or renovation projects seem to be easy ways to put STM groups to work. If you are doing a building project, perhaps you can help fund the hiring of someone from the community and come alongside that person (or company) by offering any labor or resources that would be helpful to them. If there is not someone qualified for the job, perhaps your expertise can be used to provide someone the opportunity for job training or an apprenticeship.

Painting or clean-up projects are perfect ways to include even young children in community efforts. Murals that involve and represent the community are much less likely to get tagged by gang graffiti than sterile walls that will constantly need to be painted over. Ownership begets pride, and a healthy type of pride in one's community promotes solidarity and growth.

Be Discerning About Food and Clothing Distribution

This point is both about not doing for someone what they can do themselves, and about celebrating the imago Dei and restoring dignity to people.

For years, our organization gave away Thanksgiving boxes to families in our community. These were well-funded by partnering churches that would donate non-perishable items and gift cards to local grocery stores redeemable for free turkeys. Volunteers and missionaries would fill the boxes and make their rounds, delivering food boxes to homes. We would be met with great joy and gratitude by many of these families.

Oftentimes, recipients were overjoyed about getting a Thanksgiving box. Sometimes, though, being given this meal seemed to be almost a source of shame, because we were taking away the opportunity for these families to provide for themselves. One missionary noted that they would often see men slip out of the room or excuse themselves whenever the boxes came around. God complexes of the rich and the marred identity of the poor continue to be perpetuated in interactions like this.

Remember that Your Role Is to Support the Long-Term Mission of the Missionaries or Organization You Are Serving With

In other words, don't be the rock stars who make their annual pit stop for a week, leaving the long-term missionaries to seem boring with little to offer. This is especially true when working with kids. STM groups are often like the grandparent or the fun aunt, who loves to swoop in and spoil the kids with candy, then leaves the parents behind with sugar highs and days of hearing little voices ask when auntie is coming back. It's great to bring new energy and fun toys to attract large crowds, but transformation and discipleship happen in the context of long-term relationships. Do everything you can to help support and strengthen those long-term relationships rather than try to win the "most popular" contest in anyone's heart.

Short-term missions should not only support existing ministries; STMs should lead to commitments to long-term missions. The majority of STMs happen where the gospel is already being shared, but that's not necessarily a bad thing. Long-term missions efforts need the help, encouragement, and reinforcements. When STMs are done well, they bring value to communities and enrich the lives of both the guests and the hosts.

Be a Life-Long Learner, Advocate, and Ally

After attending a conference during college, a friend asked me how it was. I gave him the standard, "It was good," to which he responded, "How did it change you? If you can't tell me how it changed you, what was so good about it?" I have remembered that question ever since. How will you be changed as a result of going on a short-term mission? It would be tragic to leave an experience like that unchanged.

Here too I will give you a couple of examples. In hopes of ending this chapter on a high note, I'll start on a low note, recounting a story about a tragic time when a group left seemingly unchanged by their time serving with us in the city.

One of the areas we ministered in was a well-known park. In the late '90s and early 2000s, MacArthur Park was infamous for its drugs, violence, murders, prostitution, and all-around crime and poverty. Unless you were willing to risk your life, you did not venture through this park after dark. There was no shortage of homeless and hungry people to feed, so every Sunday afternoon we would have an outdoor "Church at the Park" service. There was a revolving door of different volunteer groups that would go and help us serve food to the homeless every week.

One year, a group from a wealthy suburban church came to the park and eagerly gave out food, toiletries, and clothes. Clearly, many people in this group were not accustomed to seeing this type of poverty face-to-face, but by the end it was evident that they felt good about helping those who were in obvious need. They seemed particularly moved by the sight of families who were poverty-stricken. It was one thing to see a homeless, intoxicated man line up to get a sandwich, but it was another to see six unkempt and hungry-looking young children trail behind their mother to get whatever food and clothes they could. Surely even the hardest of hearts would feel some compassion toward hungry children. In the moment, everyone did.

Much to our dismay, however, not long after that church group had returned home, our ministry got an angry letter that said that their church would not be continuing to support our ministry. It turns out that at some point during the trip, perhaps during the debrief of their time in the park, one of the missionaries had mentioned that many of the people in that neighborhood were undocumented immigrants—"undocumented" in our words, "illegal" in theirs. Regardless of how or why or when these undocumented people had gotten there, for many people from this visiting church, "the law is the law" and if your papers are not current, you are in violation of the law and should not be in the U.S. For them, continuing to financially support and partner with our organization meant they were supporting unlawful behavior and not obeying the law of the land.

Just a little bit of time and distance away from their encounters in the park were enough to turn their hearts back, and they resumed blindly following the letter of the law over the spirit of the law. This is why I think it is important to constantly ask God to give us "eyes to see, ears to hear, and the courage to obey." I truly wonder how people in this group would answer the clichéd question, "What would Jesus do?"

And now to end on a high note, I'll highlight some ways that STMs have had an immeasurable eternal impact. There are too many stories to recount here and many stories that have not yet been told. I've chosen to share this one, though, because it has a bit of a twist.

The teens I ministered to were often the ones who "received" from STM groups. They were used to seeing groups come and go and some of them experienced this sort of short-term missionary engagement from a very young age. In high school they begin to register that they are perceived to be the "have nots," the "under-privileged," or the "under-resourced." Marred identity can really start to take root at this age.

To help combat this marred identity in our teens, our youth ministry team (consisting of me and three volunteers) created a leadership development program. We worked with a group of teens over the course of a year to help develop leadership skills. Weekly attendance and the fulfillment of certain criteria were required to participate in a weeklong short-term mission trip of our own.

Every August, the teens who successfully completed our leadership development program joined us on a trip to San Francisco/Oakland to serve at our organization's ministry site there. Much like other STM groups, we put on Vacation Bible School-type programs, helped out in food pantries, did clean-up projects, helped clean out churches, and served food to the homeless. One boast-worthy element of the trip was that we got to do a historical tour of the birthplace of the Black Panther Party. We walked the neighborhoods that they aimed to protect (from police brutality) and learned about the Black Panther Party's value of serving the poor and empowering the people. It was a very different narrative than the reputation they acquired for being violent revolutionaries. Particularly for our black youth, there was something very redemptive about that historical tour.

The moment that I want to highlight here, though, is when one of our teens, Cesar, prayed with a young boy to commit his life to Jesus. The teens had prepared a VBS program for thirty to fifty kids that week, and we were told by our hosts that we could expect that many kids to show up at the food bank distribution pantry. For whatever reason, eight-year-old Isaiah was the *only* kid who showed up all three days. Needless to say, he went home with lots of snacks and prizes. Our team of ten youth played games with him, did crafts with him, and did all they could to entertain and love on Isaiah. Because they chose to modify the program to suit one child, they never included an "altar response"-type time and we almost made the mistake of sending Isaiah away without the chance to commit his life to Jesus. After three days of a VBS program, Cesar simply asked eight-year-old Isaiah if he'd ever prayed about following Jesus. For some reason it had never occurred to anyone else to have this conversation. Cesar saw the missing piece and prayed what he said felt like a very genuine prayer with Isaiah, and we all celebrated a life given to Jesus for eternity. It was particularly celebratory because Cesar was the leader-in-training who struggled the most throughout the year. He was constantly late, forgetting about assignments and meetings to the point that I finally told him if he missed or was late to one more thing he would not be joining us in San Francisco. Cesar was the first one to every meeting after that conversation.

We went on our STM trip in August. In early October, Cesar came down with a fever. What was incorrectly diagnosed as walking pneumonia turned out to be meningitis. Cesar died the next day. His death came as a shock to all of us. As we all took time to remember our friend and share stories about Cesar, everyone on that trip was so grateful for the opportunity to celebrate Cesar leading Isaiah to faith in Christ. This was part of young fifteen-year-old Cesar's legacy, and that STM to the Bay is one we will never forget.

FINAL THOUGHTS

I pray that if you choose to participate in a short-term mission trip in the city (and I hope you will), it will open up your eyes to things you've never seen or understood before. And as you catch a glimpse of things as they are, both the beautiful and the broken, I pray you will become more deeply committed to working toward a greater expression of shalom in urban neighborhoods. In whatever places of power and influence you hold, I pray you will use your position to help make wrong things right even if it costs you comfort, time, and money. Each of us carries the image of God, and if you are a committed follower of Jesus you have the power of the Holy Spirit and the calling to make the world a better place. May you be constant and unwavering in submitting yourself to the leading and direction of the Holy Spirit. *Vaya con Dios.*

RESPONSE

KURT RIETEMA

There is so much I have to commend in this chapter. Susie does a masterful job in providing practical advice to infuse intercultural awareness into the planning and facilitation of short-term missions. She highlights some of the differences in culture that participants in short-term missions might encounter and helps us to understand that *different does not equal bad*. We must not conflate the two. This is good advice to enhance the cultural intelligence of anyone going on short-term missions.

But I think Susie and I are actually calling for something more than cultural intelligence. I think cultural intelligence is helpful so that we do not offend our hosts. When we get it right, knowing the histories and values that give rise to habits and practices different from ours can help us further our objectives and make our work in—to use Susie's example—backyard Bible Clubs more impactful. However, what I believe Susie and I are both advocating for is another kind of intelligence—one through which it's understood that it is more important for us to look at the *systems* of inequality than the *symptoms* that result from it. Too often, Christians are doing the downstream work of rescuing drowning swimmers rather than trying to figure out who upstream is pushing them into the river. We can't pretend to love our oppressed neighbors if we refuse to face the people, the policies, and the ideologies that oppress them. Sometimes that means confronting the uncomfortable truth of our own complicity.

Where I want to invite others to take one step further from what Susie has presented here is in the dichotomy we too often place between the work of alleviating injustice and the gospel. Susie flirts with the kind of theology that is capable of bridging this divide but I think the chapter lands short. I find this evidenced by what is ultimately celebrated at the end of the chapter—a prayer for conversion. Perhaps Susie is merely being coy because she knows the audience better than I do. But it's my belief that we do not seek to eradicate poverty because it gives credibility to our message. We do not confront our attachments to materialism because they are barriers in our relationship to God. We do not face the legacy of white supremacy because it is a black eye on the witness of the evangelical church in America. We don't do these things because they are mere tools or strategies that facilitate our sharing of the gospel. We do these things because *they are the gospel.* We do these things because justice and love overflow from the very character and constitution of the God of the universe. Jesus has brought near those who were once excluded from citizenship in Israel. Jesus has proclaimed good news to the poor, freedom for those facing mass incarceration, recovery of sight for the blind, and freedom for the oppressed. The good news is that we are no longer foreigners or strangers, but we are radically, audaciously called *God's very children*—daughters and sons! The good news is that in God's household, the King desires that each and every princess and prince lacks nothing, that their cups might overflow.

Last week, I took a short-term missions group to a migrant shelter on the Mexican side of the border and for hours listened to the stories of mothers leaving behind absolutely everything they had known because they would do *anything*, they would go to *any lengths*, to protect their kids and to recapture at least a shadow of the life they had once had before it was taken from them. This is precisely the love of Christ that Paul wrote about to the Ephesians. As God's daughters and sons, God will go to any lengths—no matter how wide and long and high and deep—to share the abundance of God's creation with those children from whom it has been withheld.

So we participate in Christ's continuing work of destroying every barrier, every dividing wall of hostility, not as something that's secondary and that paves the way for others to make prayers that echo into eternity. We do it because when we do it is the very kind of *salvation* that Jesus proclaimed had come to the house of Zacchaeus after providing restitution to victims of economic predation. Let's celebrate any kind of conversion from a life hoarded out of fear that there will never be enough to one extravagantly shared because of a trust in God's generous abundance. Let's praise these conversions just as enthusiastically as Jesus did. Justice isn't a tool. It isn't a concession to popular cultural and political movements. Seeking the equitable distribution of an abundant creation is the loving impulse of a loving God for beloved children.

VIEW 4:
ALLEVIATING PRIVILEGE THROUGH SHORT-TERM MISSIONS

BY KURT RIETEMA

INTRODUCTION

Paul. We like to think of him as the poster boy for short-term missions. Paul—the one whose passport had been inked in Iconium, who took selfies in Salamus, made disciples in Derbe, not to mention sported matching T-shirts with Timothy. Just imagine the church slideshow back in Antioch showing a pic of Paul with a viper clinging to his wrist like a fake Rolex. But before Paul ever set sail over the Mediterranean or clambered through the Macedonian countryside, he set out on a different kind of mission trip to Damascus. We then knew him as Saul, and Saul wasn't so friendly with the locals.

Saul believed he was on a mission from God to set the wayward of Damascus straight. He went there to stamp out erroneous beliefs that were spreading like an outbreak of the measles from a nondescript upper room in Jerusalem. It was a noble purpose, really. Saul's intentions were good. And so were those of the rest of the religious inner circle. They wanted to save others from going down a wrong road that would not only be destructive to them personally, but corrosive to Jews as a whole.

The burden to show backwards people the right way of believing and behaving falls to pedigreed people like Saul—those with top-notch,

Gamalielan educations, those from good, well-connected, Benjamite families, and those whose religious reputations were above reproach. So, Saul went on his mission to Damascus not only with the full backing of the religious authorities, but also, he believed, with the support and commission of the God of the universe. Little did Saul know that the one God sought to convert wasn't among the frail and frightened people of Damascus, but the missionary himself.

We know the rest of the story. Jesus met Saul in a dramatic fashion. "Saul, Saul, why do you persecute me?" As if the hypnotic, '90s laser show on the Damascus road wasn't frightening enough, imagine the complete bewilderment and utter disbelief Saul must have been going through at that moment. Saul could agree that he was, in fact, persecuting Jesus and his cronies. Jesus was the cause of this outbreak in the first place. But what Saul couldn't get his mind around was the fact that Jesus was the God-in-flesh that the backwards people claimed him to be. The floor of Saul's world had collapsed underneath him. He, Saul—the good, the educated, the religious, the zealous— was not the defender of God and God's people that he'd supposed himself to be. Instead, Jesus made the accusation that Saul was his very opposite. Saul was the oppressor.

While we're all familiar with Saul's encounter with Jesus on the Damascus road, we often overlook his second encounter at the house of Judas, this one with Ananias, which made Saul's conversion complete. Saul's first encounter with Jesus provoked a crisis. It created a rupture with his past. Saul could no longer return to who he once was and what he once did. For three days Saul was left disoriented and confused, with no appetite save for answers about what might come next. It was Saul's encounter with Ananias that provided the answer to his crisis.

While Saul's encounter with Jesus showed him who he could no longer be, his encounter with Ananias showed Saul who he now needed to be. Saul's mission was to enact and proclaim among all people the relational reorientation that the Spirit instigated between him and Ananias. Saul's mission was to reveal Christ's purpose to create in himself one new humanity. To proclaim that the old barriers

and dividing walls of hostility had been destroyed. That in Christ
Jesus, labels of Jew and Gentile, slave and free, male and female,
barbarian and Scythian—all of the rules that once separated and
segregated us had been repealed and replaced. It wasn't that those
identities were erased and no longer mattered. It's that in Christ, the
power those divisions had to exclude, to dominate and oppress, had
been defeated. Saul was to reintroduce the estranged children of God
to one another, reuniting them as long-lost brothers and sisters who
had finally come home. The Spirit had commissioned Saul with the
ministry of reconciliation.

What if this were the purpose of short-term missions? What if
short-term missions weren't about well-educated, well-adjusted,
well-connected, and well-funded youth going to poor, "backwards"
communities to win them over to their spiritual and cultural beliefs
and behaviors, but about young people coming face-to-face with the
humanity, the warmth, and the extravagant generosity of those who
have been dehumanized? What if we released ourselves of the burden
to save, to fix, to "fulfill" the Great Commission, to end poverty, or
to make an impact, and instead entertained the idea that, like Saul,
it might just be us who need saving? What if we need to traverse
borders—whether that border is the Rio Grande or the fence around
our subdivision—because whether we're conscious of it or not, we are
homesick for one another? What if for one week, our unconscious
ache, the groaning of all creation for the sons and daughters of God
to be revealed, finds its consolation? And what if there we catch a
glimpse of a world unbroken, where the rent fabric of our tribalized
lives is momentarily stitched back together again and we mend the
tears that have severed us from one another? What if this is what
short-term missions could look like?

MY PRIORITIES

I'd like for us to consider a different starting point for short-term
missions. This framework is guided by three main priorities. The first
begins with the action of God. What we find in the gospels is a God
who entered into the pain and heartache of a broken world to be with

God's children. We witness a Jesus who constantly transgressed the social boundaries of his day in order to come near to those who had been left out. Jesus disrupted patterns of power and turned the logic of the world on its head, proclaiming that the first shall be last and the last shall be first and enacting that new reality with his disciples. And when the Spirit descended on Pentecost, the disciples were only beginning a long journey to grasp just how wide and long and high and deep is the love of Christ. Sorcerers from Samaria, eunuchs from Ethiopia, paralytics from Lydda, centurions from Caesarea—no one was outside the orbit of God's field of gravity. God's Spirit was taking them to places and breaking down barriers so unfathomable that they had to assemble a conference in Jerusalem just to compare notes. They were quite literally building an entire library, a veritable canon of experiences and testimonies of God creating one new humanity out of the two, thus making peace.

If the first priority is about God's desire to create one new humanity, the second is related. It is the groundwork that must precede the reconstruction. In order to create one new humanity, we must first identify and name the dividing walls that nearly two thousand years later still stand between us. We must confess that our identities as Jew and Gentile, male and female, white and black, rich and poor, Republican and Democrat, citizen and immigrant, still wield their dark, ancient powers. Inequality robs so many of God's children of full access and enjoyment of the material abundance of God's creation. For those of us who benefit materially from inequality, we are robbed spiritually. Our consciences are blunted as we "turn away from our own flesh and blood" (Isaiah 58:7), as we explain away and theologize our privilege and others' impoverishment under the guise of God's blessing. Like Cain, we deny that we are our brothers' keepers. We deny we're brothers and sisters at all.

It is as if, to borrow Dr. King's famous metaphor, Christ signed a promissory note guaranteeing that the barriers have been destroyed, but we have defaulted on this promissory note. In the divided and splintered society we inhabit, we have now come to cash a check for the one new humanity that Christ has guaranteed. It's our task to take up the arduous work of making real—to enact and make manifest among us—what Christ has made possible.

My third priority in framing short-term missions is to develop an awareness that the dividing walls of humanity are upheld and reinforced by those who seek to benefit the most from them. Black Americans did not choose to sequester themselves into districts where they could not access bank loans, where schools were underfunded, where they were sometimes victims of over-policing and sometimes victims of under-policing. Whites redlined black people there and created racially-restrictive covenants to keep them out of their own neighborhoods. Indigenous peoples did not choose to move to tribal reservations. The U.S. government reluctantly ceded the leftover lands, the crumbs from the table of colonial settlement, after breaking treaty upon treaty. Refugees do not choose their camps, nor do immigrants choose their detention centers. They don't leave behind friends and family, food, landscape, ritual, and belonging out of envy for the riches and lifestyles of the West. We create these places to corral those who have suffered violence, to conceal our own complicity, to contain them from sharing in any part of that which we believe is ours. The privilege of some is often bound up with the impoverishment of others.

If we are to create a new humanity and dismantle the dividing walls, we must recognize that the lion's share of this work is on those who benefit from the barriers. Justice is first and foremost an act of relinquishment by the powerful, rather than a required change in the behavior of the vulnerable. Israel's exodus out of Egypt was premised on Pharaoh begrudgingly letting God's people go, not the enslaved people's lack of desire for freedom. Although both Saul and Ananias had to renegotiate the ways in which they thought of and related to one another, it was Saul who had the most drastic changes to make. Conversion was painful. Saul had to deal with the disorientation he felt when Jesus revealed that he and the people he thought of as good, decent, God-loving folks were not the victims in the story. They were the villains.

If it isn't clear by now, the framework I'm suggesting for short-term missions isn't one for all times, all people, and all places. Not all of those going on short-term missions are people of privilege, nor would the majority of them think of themselves as such. However, the participant data and the average cost of short-term mission trips demonstrates that short-term missions are extravagant endeavors accessible only to those with relative levels of privilege.[1,2] By and large, short-term missions are the activity of the affluent for the affluent. Because short-term missions are often marketed as poverty alleviation, others have called their proponents' bluff. They've called for a moratorium on these short-term missions because if it's truly more about helping those in poverty than the goers' adventures in altruism, it's a terribly wasteful and inefficient strategy. Yet in my experience, privileged people seldom give up their privileges voluntarily. That includes the privilege of travel to impoverished areas.

Perhaps, then, we need to call it like it is. Short-term mission trips are for the people going on them. But like we see in Jesus's encounter with Saul, we make it our priority to "convert" the would-be missionaries to the interests of those who have been oppressed. Like Saul, perhaps our work on short-term missions is to wrestle with the weight of our own complicity. It's learning to slowly let go of the advantages that have accumulated in our favor for the sake of our brothers and sisters who have been disadvantaged. It's recognizing that Christians are not to be threatened by the laying aside of our power. Nor are we afraid or dismissive of conversations about checking our privilege, because Christ first showed us the way. It was Christ who being in the very nature God did not consider equality with God as something to be used to his own advantage, but instead took on the very nature of a servant—a slave, the lowest position in society.

In reimagined short-term missions, young people do not travel "downwards" from places of privilege to places of impoverishment in order to change others, but to be changed by them. They go not as saviors, but as servants. They go not to teach, but to be taught. They go not to demonstrate hard work, to teach personal responsibility, or to teach how to keep one's loose pants from sagging. Their work is to soften their own hard hearts. To be responsible for opening their own closed minds. To loosen their own clenched fists. They go to practice humility and the valuing of others above themselves. To look not to their own interests, but to the interests of others. To learn to lay aside their privileges so that the underprivileged might have their share. The author of Hebrews writes, "And so Jesus also suffered outside the city gate to make the people holy through his own blood. Let us, then, go to him outside the camp, bearing the disgrace he bore" (Hebrews 13:12-13). He suggests that the face of Christ is still there—outside the camp, outside of the protections, the belonging, the citizenship that many enjoy. Perhaps this is why we go on short-term missions. We are compelled to go outside the city gate. We leave our subdivisions, our rural towns, to go outside the camp because the blood, the pain, and the sacrifices of some lives for the sake of others are still being offered. We go to the public housing projects and the Bantustans of apartheid South Africa because the plunder and pillaging of others' lives happens at a distance. We go, if only for a week, to bear the disgrace they bear, to enjoin our lives with the children of God whose lives have been upended by their exclusion.

MY APPROACH

To construct a different approach to short-term missions, let's consider an experience that might lend itself as a metaphor. I recently began watching a nature series that, like others, has breathtaking cinematography that captures the wild wonder and beauty of God's created world.[3] Unlike other nature documentaries, it doesn't protect its viewers from nor make discreet references about the threat of climate change. It makes the connections explicit. It is not blasé about the effects of a changing planet. Rather, it communicates to the broader public the sense of urgency that the overwhelming body of scientific research has been warning us about. Yet it does it not through the alarming statistics that keep climatologists and entomologists awake at night, but by bringing us up close and intimate with the animals and the landscapes that are disappearing.

I'd heard of ocean rise caused by Arctic ice melt before, but it's always felt so distant. The time horizon for any catastrophic consequences feels so far removed. What's more, living in middle America makes me even more ambivalent about the effects of ocean rise. Yet even if I lived on a coast, to imagine that something happening in the Arctic could have an effect on me, thousands of miles away, might feel as far off and fantastical a fairytale as one about the elves who run Santa's workshop there. While I'm no climate denier, in terms of how much I've allowed my belief in climate change to adjust my habits and behaviors, I'm the environmentalist's equivalent of the guy who shows up to church on Christmas and Easter. I've got my Sierra Club lifetime membership card, but I can guarantee you no one at the local chapter knows my name.

Yet something happened to me while watching this documentary. One of the most spectacular and terrifying moments occurred when a camera hovered over the edge of an ice shelf when suddenly, seventy-five million tons of ice broke off in a cataclysmic calving of a glacier. The scale of the glacier's collapse was incomprehensible. A hunk of ice the size of a skyscraper fell into the ocean and the heaving of more than a quarter mile of the iceberg hidden beneath the waters came crashing through the surface and created tidal waves several stories high in its displacement. The groaning of all of creation was unveiled in a way I could not turn away from, nor could I do anything to stop. I could only bear witness to it. In bearing witness, the calving of the glacier unsettled me and roused me from my complacency toward our hurting planet like nothing I had ever seen or heard before.

Let's consider the value of my mediated encounter with a calving glacier for a moment. The first achievement the directors accomplished was to close the distance between me and the far-off phenomena of Arctic melting. By bringing the viewer to the edge of the ice face as the floor fell from beneath it, the *geographic*, *temporal*, and *empathic* distance was diminished. It felt near, it felt urgent. It became something personally valuable to me that the world is losing.

Second, I bore witness to broken creation, and the truth about what has been occurring was told in a way that I could not deny. Question the science if you will, downplay humanity's role in climate change, but this cannot erase the unsettling experience of witnessing an iceberg plunge into the frigid waters below.

Third, the abstraction of climate change was made real and personal. The grim statistics of global warming—as startling as they are—had done little to galvanize me into action. Yet, when I watched the moment of collapse I found myself caught up in the story of one glacier's death and demise. My head had all of the knowledge it needed to convince me climate change was real. It was my heart that hadn't yet compelled me to action.

Fourth, the directors won me over through beauty, not through guilt or scare tactics. I was enraptured by a polar bear and her cubs and caught up by the immense power and fragility of the Arctic. Their beauty had a gravity. Its magnetism attracted rather than repelled. Their beauty provided a compass, a direction to move toward rather than run from.

Lastly, the directors connected the dots between the symptoms of climate change and the systems that are causing it. I was humbled by my own smallness. There was nothing that I, sitting at home watching, nor the cinematographers nor the directors on location, could do to stop this from happening. It irreversibly happened, it is irreversibly happening, and it will continue to happen for the foreseeable future unless we make drastic changes. The solution to Arctic melting is not a localized one. The local site of the glacial calving is merely where the symptoms of a more systemic, global problem are revealed. The change needed is in the common behaviors and the habits of everyday people like me and in the policies of powerful corporations and governments thousands of miles away.

I want us to consider how we might frame a young person's encounter with a community experiencing poverty on short-term missions with the same intention that the directors of the nature documentary gave to my encounter with a glacier melting and calving icebergs. Let's map out a different approach to short-term missions using five takeaways from the nature documentary and overlay that with insights drawn from Saul's encounter with Ananias. Then we'll bring in other stories to add texture as well as a few practical ways to implement change.

Here is the approach that we're going to take:
1. Close the distance.
2. Bear witness.
3. Make abstractions real and personal.
4. Let beauty persuade.
5. Connect symptoms to systems.

Close the Distance

Susan Sontag, in her book *Regarding the Pain of Others*, writes about the role of photography as a means of making "real" that which we might prefer to ignore—most specifically, war. War, like other hostilities that disproportionately affect vulnerable people, is waged at a distance. Photographs have a way of closing that distance and forcing us to reckon with its violence. "Look, the photographs say, *this* is what it's like. This is what war *does*. And *that*, that is what it does, too. War tears, rends. War rips open, eviscerates. War scorches. War dismembers. War *ruins*," Sontag writes.[4] The directors of the nature documentary understood this. They intended the calving glacier to have the same emotional effect. To take us on a journey to the places where the effects of a warming planet are most explicit. To unveil the hidden violence. *This* is what it's like. This is what climate change does. Proximity increases our sense of responsibility to act. When the problems of others are out of sight and out of mind, we're not even bystanders anymore. We're complete strangers to their plight. But the closer that we get, the harder it is to ignore the crimes happening to others.

What if we understood short-term missions as a way of closing the gap between young people who are unaware of or complacent about the injustices their estranged brothers and sisters face? Perhaps it's helpful to think of short-term missions as a new "technology" for closing this geographic, temporal, and empathic distance. The technology of the printing press democratized the Bible by putting God's Word into the hands of the laity, subverting the officially-sanctioned readings of the papacy. The dissemination of photographs and film documenting the atrocities of the Vietnam

War created a populist backlash against Washington's war doctrine. The proliferation of drone video and streaming services can now take millions to the epicenter of global climate change, graphically conveying its bleeding heart. Likewise, the technology that makes available discounted international airfare has made travel accessible, particularly to places where the public has been sold stories of corrupt leaders, failed states, and cultures of poverty. But what happens to these sanctioned narratives when more young people take up this new technology that closes the distance between them and people who experience that pain firsthand? What unvarnished, unflattering truths about themselves and their beloved institutions might be unearthed? What fissures in their beliefs about our own exceptionalism and the righteousness of our national presence on the global stage might begin to form because of their encounters there?

Because our world is so segregated, so diced and julienned into lifestyle enclaves and mobile home parks, we need mechanisms to help us see. Until Dr. King's dream of little black boys and girls holding hands with little white boys and girls becomes a normal, accepted part of our American landscape, we need staged, prosthetic means to bridge the divides. It will not happen organically. It will not happen through good intentions. Our struggle is not against flesh and blood. There are powers and principalities that are deeply invested in our division and we must not discount them, thinking we can overcome these obstacles through ordinary means. We need the extraordinary. We need the shock and awe of the Damascus road. We need the Lord literally calling out to us in visions, because under no uncertain terms would Saul otherwise have coffee with the apostles, nor Ananias visit the house of his oppressor. We need some kind of artificial scaffolding. We need pathways back to one another. We need imported technologies like short-term missions to put us in the same space together and to be in relationship with the other.

Bear Witness

The formerly-enslaved person turned abolitionist and preacher Frederick Douglass said that whenever he saw some terrible denunciation of slavery in the papers, he read them enthusiastically. In his autobiography Douglass notes, "I had a deep satisfaction in the thought that the rascality of slaveholders was not concealed from the eyes of the world, and that I was not alone in abhorring the cruelty and brutality of slavery."[5] While no Northerner could ever understand the living hells that he and other enslaved persons endured, there was comfort in the fact that they shared Douglass's outrage. What was happening in the South was no secret and though separated by distance, he and other enslaved persons weren't the only soldiers, nor theirs the only battlefields in the war against slavery.

I think one of the values of short-term missions approached in this way is in the sense of solidarity that it might offer to those facing injustice. To know that they are not alone. That the rascality of their oppressors in not concealed.

René August, an Anglican priest who grew up as a young black girl in apartheid South Africa, talks about short-term missions in terms of pilgrimage. René will often take groups to Robben Island, where Nelson Mandela was held prisoner. She says that Robben Island has a kind of power: "It cracks you open." There are certain places that open you up, and we can use this openness to take young people on a deeper, more introspective journey to map out their own social locations; to help them understand the ways in which they have been unknowing, passive beneficiaries of unjust systems. I've been with short-term groups in Jamaican fields where slaves once cut sugarcane, infirmaries where the elderly and deformed are discarded, a site in my own neighborhood where the famous Shawnee chief Tecumseh's brother once lived, warning through prophetic visions not to trust white settlers. I've walked the streets of Ferguson where Mike Brown's body lay on the streets for hours, and I've visited the room in the Lorraine Motel where Dr. King was assassinated. The stories exhumed in these places have a haunting power that cracks us open. This is what it means to bear witness.

Bearing witness is a quiet work. It's not something that we do, but rather something done unto us. Our "work" is simply to pay attention and to not turn away. Just as being overcome by the sheer scale of the collapse of ice, perhaps the "work" of short-term missions is to bear witness to the systemic collapse of opportunity people in that community face. To allow the weight of it to break us open like Saul's encounter with Jesus on the Damascus road.

Yet too often, we give young people the impression that the problems they encounter in communities suffering from inequality are things that can be fixed by their hands. This coincides with a trend in short-term missions to center the needs of the local community rather than the needs and desires of outside visitors. This has, for the most part, been a helpful corrective. We must be adamant about not inflicting trauma on locals in the name of educating far more privileged young people. Locals are not there as props to enhance outsiders' experiences or their adventures in altruism. But I wonder if saying "it's not about us, it's about them" is a convenient way of removing ourselves from the equation of inequality. When we focus on helping, we get to be heroes. And by making ourselves the heroes, we erase our names from the list of suspects.

What if we unapologetically said these trips have always been *for* us, but we reframe the reasons why we center the visiting groups? Like Arctic melting, the solutions to the problems marginalized people face are not localized ones. Under-resourced communities are only the sites where the symptoms of much broader systemic injustices are revealed. Ananias's problem wasn't within his capacity to change. It was Saul's anxiety about a religious sect that followed Jesus. It was Saul's misguided belief in the righteousness of his mission. It was Saul's abuse of power legitimized by the religious authorities through sanctioned means that killed Stephen. While Ananias certainly loosened his shoulders after he laid his hands on Saul, the central character of God's transformative work in their shared encounter was the outsider visiting.

Make Abstractions Real and Personal

For Saul, Ananias was just an abstraction. The followers of Jesus were lawbreakers, pure and simple. Ananias had already been safely categorized and branded a heretic in Saul's mind. He didn't need to see Ananias's humanity because he believed Ananias had already surrendered his right to it. Then Saul was blind and begging for answers and Ananias showed up knocking at his door. It was quite possibly the first time Saul had actually met a Christian—at least, one who wasn't under interrogation.

The neighborhood I live in is largely a working-class poor, Latino neighborhood. Men are in construction, landscaping, and warehouse jobs. Women work as maids, house cleaners, line cooks, and fruit packers. Many are immigrants, a significant portion of whom are undocumented. For many Americans, this is the only way that they relate to immigrants—as functionaries who carry out essential services. Immigrants are valuable to them inasmuch as they supply a steady source of cheap labor. Shane Claiborne once wrote, "I had come to see that the great tragedy of the church is not that rich Christians do not care about the poor but that rich Christians do not know the poor."[6] The same can be said about immigrants. By and large, they are an abstraction to most Americans.

One of the reasons I host short-term missions groups in our neighborhood is to change this equation. Yes, we spend a few hours of our day doing the typical service stuff—painting a neighbor's house, helping out at food banks, sorting clothes at thrift stores. But at least one night during the week, we split into groups and share meals in our neighbors' homes. When we do this, the power dynamic changes. The young people are no longer the givers, they're the receivers. My immigrant friends are no longer the anonymous workers who cut their parents' grass, who bus their volleyball team's tables, who launder the sheets at their vacation rental. They're Cristina. Alejandro. Lorena. Beto. They're no longer faceless criminals who care little about the rule of law. They're the mother who, for the past six years, calls her kids in Mexico every day so they can do homework together over the phone. They're fathers who've left everything for the sake of their families. They've missed birthdays and *quinceañeras,* trying not to lie to themselves again: "Just one more year and I'll be home." Something happens when you're put in a room with people you're not used to being with and you share an experience around food, laughter, and stories. Scales fall from their eyes, I swear it. The Spirit sets the stage and a whole new world, a whole new way of seeing, opens up for them.

Let Beauty Persuade

Shortly after the 2016 election, Amina Amdeen, who is Muslim, marched with other University of Texas students to protest the election of Donald Trump. However, not all who were present that day felt the same way about the president as Amdeen and her friends did. Joseph Weidknecht showed up as a counterprotestor wearing a "Make America Great Again" hat. It was a peaceful protest, but then hostility began. Amdeen noticed some of her fellow protestors surrounding the Trump supporter and threatening him. Someone took his red hat. As she later tells Weidknecht in an interview, "And that's the point where I…something kind of snapped inside of me because I wear a Muslim hijab and I've been in situations where people have tried to snatch it off my head. And I rushed towards you and I just started screaming 'Leave him alone! Give me that back!'" In the rush of an instant, something happened between these two, who, in Weidknecht's own words, could not be any further apart as people. The young Muslim girl saw one of the most intimate, personal expressions of her Muslim faith—her hijab—in one of the most notorious symbols of a political movement, a movement in which anti-Muslim factions would eagerly snatch away her right to wear her hijab. Later in the interview, Weidknecht confesses to Amdeen, "You are genuinely the only Muslim person I know. It is not that I have actively avoided, it's just, I've just never been in a position, where I can interact for an extended period of time. So, I guess my views on the Muslim community have been influenced by a lot of the news articles and things of that nature."[7]

Amdeen does what, according to the fixed stereotype in Weidknecht's mind, runs contrary to the very essence of what it means to be Muslim. The infidel comes to the defense of the patriot. Weidknecht had no categories for this. In the hour of his need, his would-be enemy doesn't just say, "knock it off, guys." She frantically rushes to his side, screaming, demanding, risking her own safety, putting her body between his and his harassers, *as if he were family*. This is what Ananias did at the house of Judas. There he performed one of the most intimate of gestures, demonstrating an exquisite, otherworldly act of grace and beauty. Ananias gently placed his hands on his oppressor and spoke these words, "*Brother* Saul." Saul's definitive story about Ananias could not weather the force of this undeserved kindness. They were no longer enemies, but estranged brothers who were beginning the beautiful but awkward process of learning to be family.

You are genuinely the only _____ person I know. Fill in the blank. There are dozens of labels we might substitute. If ever there's a time when we need to create pathways back to one another, that time is now. It's killing us not to have spaces where people can interact with others not like them for extended periods of time. We can't see past stereotypes because we haven't had intimate enough experiences with the other to subvert them.

Jesus could have personally turned Saul around and given him a fresh start. But he chose not to do it alone. Instead, God enlisted Ananias's help. Perhaps it's because Saul needed to see the humanity of those he'd persecuted. Saul needed to feel and know up close the kind, caring, undeserved, grace-filled touch of the one he had oppressed. And by this Saul was healed. On the short-term missions groups I lead, I enlist coconspirators from among my neighbors and friends to be Ananias for the young people. Some of my friends are cognizant of their role. They know where the young people come from. They know how these young people's communities think about immigrants, about people in poverty. We talk about it. They know what's at stake. Other friends don't understand the full picture of what we're trying to do, but they don't care. Regardless, they don't participate reluctantly. Hospitality is simply who they are. They win young people over with love. These neighbors and friends defy expectations through sharing life as their little kids parade black belts in taekwondo and through transcendent plates of *puerco en salsa verde*. I can't tell you how many complete strangers my friends have invited to their daughters' *quinceañeras*, wearing down any stubborn residues of distrust while line dancing to endless stanzas of *Caballo Dorado*.

Those of us who care about justice are often tempted to resort to anger. When we take seriously the idea that every human being is a child who is as fiercely loved by their Father as we love our own children, that anger is not without warrant. We don't blame Ananias for his resistance to God's command. He had every reason in the world to say, "No way. Not him." Nevertheless, we must remember that change has a critical pathway and it doesn't begin with our heads. It begins with our hearts. There is a logical flowchart to this work. The softening of hearts is the key to unlocking closed minds. The reverse is rarely true. Order matters. We can't speak the truth without first speaking love. Perfect love drives out fear. Laughter breaks the hardest of hearts. Let the beauty of locals' lives and the magnetism of their humanity draw young people out of their complacency. Let the stories of newly-named brothers and sisters give young people direction, purpose, and the spiritual drive to bring heaven on earth for their siblings.

Connect Symptoms to Systems

The encounters young people have with my neighbors crush them with kindness, with simple acts of beauty, of extravagant hospitality and generosity. When the Spirit turns them toward one another and they're reoriented as family, the pain and injustices their friends face become personal. It isn't random cruelty affecting anonymous people in some faraway place. It's injustice against people they care about in a place they've given a piece of their heart. Only then are they open enough, only then are their hearts soft enough, only then do they have the ears to hear the reasons why their friends are stuck.

The foreclosure crisis upended the entire block in the low-income neighborhood where we live. In the aftermath of evictions, as the dust settled and prices dropped, outside investors—the only ones with any capital left—were there to snatch up houses for a song. My wife and I created a small social enterprise by accident. We began helping immigrant families purchase these homes through low-interest, private financing after we saw so many of our friends and neighbors get taken advantage of. We found ourselves bidding against these outside investors, sometimes winning, sometimes losing. On a few occasions, I had the opportunity to meet these investors. One had outbid us and purchased a house across the street from us for $18,000.

One day I introduced myself to tell him about our immigrant

neighbors, and to offer him a quick profit of a few thousand dollars without putting any work into the house by selling it to me as-is. He was exceptionally nice and amicable. We shared the same home state, cheered for the same alma mater. He was even friends with a distant cousin of mine. He was just a middle-aged white man from the suburbs diversifying his investment portfolio so he could send his daughter to the same college I went to. He declined my offer to purchase the home, but suggested he could personally finance for the friends we'd hoped would be able to live in this house. These former neighbors of ours had lost their home to foreclosure a few years prior. A week later, he shared the terms. Over the course of fifteen years, his $18,000 investment would have amounted to my friends paying him over $150,000. This arrangement was no anomaly. Good, well-intentioned people from the same walks of life as us take advantage of vulnerable people in low-income neighborhoods over and over and over under the innocent guise of investment. This is the banality of evil. We forget that the wolf doesn't always dress in wolves' clothing. His respectability is finely tailored. His work ethic is clean cut. His churchgoing is perfectly matched to his love for his own children.

This is what we do when we host short-term missions groups. We show them around the neighborhood to see beyond the surface. We tell them these stories. We make visible the invisible powers and principalities. We uncover the hidden violence done in the name of business, absolved by the priests of profit, in full accordance with the morality of the market because they can always find innocent people who will pay the sticker price.

On another day we take our short-term missions groups on a driving tour of Kansas City across the dividing lines of racial segregation, seeing in real time the disparities inscribed in space by manicured lawns on one block and boarded-up windows the next. These groups learn the history of redlining, blockbusting, and racially-restrictive covenants. They discover that concentrations of poverty coincide with concentrations of black families, not by accident and not by preference, but by design, codified and enforced through legal and extralegal means.

On another day, young people receive identity cards with brief bios of people from Mexico, the Philippines, and the Netherlands, all of people wanting to immigrate to the U.S. for differing reasons. They go through a simulated visa application process and see the disparities. Even aspiring, educated, bilingual immigrants like my Mexican coworker intending to leverage his own mom's U.S. citizenship have an estimated sixty-seven year wait to immigrate legally. Those who are wealthy and educated have wait times that American youth can hardly believe. Those who are poor and uneducated will wait endlessly because there's no line for them at all. We compare the restrictions our immigrant ancestors faced with those faced today. The young people on these mission trips realize that the magnanimous hospitality inscribed in the Statue of Liberty's invitation—for "your tired, your poor, your huddled masses yearning to breathe free"—is incongruent with the actual policies we have in place.

For us, connecting the symptoms of injustice to the systems that produce injustices is essential. Many short-term missions experiences bring young people into relationship with those who are different from them. But too many of those young people walk away from their experiences believing that poverty is just an unfortunate accident— as natural as glaciers breaking apart. The extreme inequalities we witness today are not natural. Inequalities are created, and they are increasing at accelerating rates. We have a responsibility on short-term missions to help young people make the connection that the inequalities they witness are often bound up with the behaviors, actions, and policies of powerful people and institutions thousands of miles away.

FINAL THOUGHTS

What God is inviting us to do through short-term missions is to widen our circle of who we love. To embrace one another as brothers and sisters, to share our resources as family and make sure none of God's kids are left out. This is not a distraction from the gospel, but the gospel's very heart. God's desire is to create one new humanity, to call every one of God's children from the far-flung corners of the earth back to God and back to each other. The Spirit will not rest until that day when all things are made new, heaven comes to earth, and every tear from every one of God's children is wiped away. Until then, God invites us to take up this good work of reconciliation because it is not a sideshow to the real work of the kingdom. Getting comfortable and learning to trust our brothers and sisters who are estranged by the corrosive sins of injustice shouldn't be a course elective. A divided country and a fragmented world groan, waiting in eager expectation for the children of God to be revealed. This work begs to be part of the core curriculum of following Jesus.

RESPONSE

JIM NOREEN

I believe that if Kurt and I were sitting down for coffee, we'd agree on a lot of things. I'd agree with him that missions should not be about "well-adjusted, well-connected, and well-funded youth going to poor, 'backwards' communities to win them over to their spiritual and cultural beliefs and behaviors." I resonate with the thought that there is one humanity, and that we are better together—as God sees us. I especially perked up at his calling out of the phrase "It's not about us, it's about them" when it comes to short-term missions. I've heard this mantra and even seen it on T-shirts, and it's never sat right. I've personally called it out to my colleagues.

That said, I believe the first part of that phrase is accurate. I believe it truly is not about "us," the mission-goers. But it's also not about "them," the local community, either. I believe missions are about "US," collectively. The church, united together as one. This is where Kurt and I might have some healthy pushback in response to each other. The approach outlined in this view unapologetically makes missions about the goer—which leads me to ask, at what point are these trips actually missions at all? Or is it that this model of missions is simply a deeper, more expensive element of discipleship?

To make missions only about the local community also has its challenges, as was outlined in Kurt's chapter. The power of missions is unleashed when both the goers and the local church serve together in unison. This opens the door for positive, lasting impact on both the missions team and the local community.

As leaders, it is our responsibility to prepare our teams. We must equip them to serve with humility and love, and—as noted in Kurt's chapter—must take the posture of learners, not teachers. The notion that an individual having been born into a privileged background renders their love, encouragement, and assistance without meaning is misleading. I do recognize that those words were not specifically written in the chapter, but one could come to that conclusion through their reading. Can we not reveal walls of injustice while at the same time utilizing a missions team's skillsets to uplift local initiatives and provide encouragement? I believe we can. I believe we can create an environment that accomplishes both—but only through partnership. This is what I'm missing the most. Where does the church play into this missions model? Pastors and local congregations have been placed in these communities with a calling to reach their communities for Christ. With short-term missions, we're bringing a potential source of encouragement and assistance to their backyards. Does the approach outlined in this chapter circumvent the local congregation's direction and dreams, while making the assumption that those participating in short-term missions are simply privileged youth who need a wake-up call?

On a recent trip to Israel, I spoke with a pastor who shared his heart regarding the thousands of Christians who visit his country each year. He was grateful that they were able to come and see the many significant sights of the Christian faith there, but I could see the discouragement in his eyes when he talked about the fact that less than 2 percent of the population of Israel follows Jesus. As thousands of Christians visit his country each year, they pass by his church (and other churches like it), eyes set on seeing those sights referenced above and deepening their faith. What if these visiting Christians, as part of their trip, chose not to pass by the local Christ-following church, but instead chose to stop there? What if they chose to listen? What if they chose to encourage and to serve? I believe that the understanding and faith of those visiting Christians would only be enriched through this experience and, at the same time, the local congregation would be seen, loved, encouraged, and assisted in ministry.

My pushback is that there's room to be intentional with both the spiritual development of the missions team and with encouraging and assisting the local church. Both elements are essential to healthy missions that make the most of what God has gifted us with. An experience was highlighted within this view where teenagers were split into groups to share meals in community members' homes. Kurt highlights the teens who, through this, experience a power dynamic change: "The Spirit sets the stage and a whole new world, a whole new way of seeing, opens up for them." Amen. Give me more of that. Rest assured, the Spirit is not only working in the hearts of those youth, but God is using that experience to work in the hearts of that household as well. Connect this spirit of humility and desire to learn with a local church, and count me in.

VIEW 5:
FROM CHARITY
TO SOLIDARITY:
DECOLONIZING SHORT-
TERM MISSIONS

BY JON HUCKINS

INTRODUCTION

I'll never forget sitting with my new friend as he looked me in the eyes to articulate the impact of short-term mission trips on his city. Luis is a Mexican pastor in Tijuana. Sitting in a home for abandoned boys that he and his family had started (and live in), there was a warmth of life and a chill of pain that ran through every breath I took. As the boys respectfully made their way from the dining room to the basketball courts, they'd give Luis a high five or bear hug. It was as sacred and as it was disorienting. A community for the hurting and the healed. The beauty and the broken. The trauma and the hope.

Before Luis ever said a word, I knew he was the real deal. Not only a trusted colleague of my dear friends, who'd introduced me to him, Luis was also someone who embodied all that I intuitively knew the gospel could look like in the world. The sacrifice and the joy inherent in the life and teachings of Jesus turned 3-D.

And then, unapologetically and graciously, he said to me, "Jon, nothing has more demobilized the Church of Tijuana than the short-term missions movement in the United States. You come down here for a week to build a house or host a Vacation Bible School and leave. We have become so dependent on your handouts that the Church of

Tijuana no longer knows how to live as the Church of Tijuana!"

I was undone.

I had been blind and Luis was helping Jesus heal my sight. I had spent so many years hiding behind my own (often well-intentioned) version of ministry success and mission trip objectives that I had completely missed the point…and directly contributed to a systemic imposition that had done more harm than good.

I grew up as part of a local church from the day I was born. Having made my way through all the children's programs, I passed through junior high ministry and had high expectations for what high school youth group would bring. Having two older sisters who had been on all the mission trips our youth ministry provided, I couldn't wait for my turn. They always came back with amazing stories, deeper friendships, and an increased gratitude for our TV.

I went on my first "Mission2Mexico" trip the summer after graduating eighth grade and returned every year for the next ten years. Throughout high school, these immersions into a different way of life, worldview, and culture—fueled by a deep conviction about the mission—were extremely formative for me. I saw, experienced, and participated in things that were so far out of my day-to-day life that I have no doubt the kingdom of God grew in diversity, richness, and beauty as a result. Lifelong friendships were made, an awareness of my inherent privilege was exposed (although we wouldn't have used those words at the time), and a view of human relationships that transcend national borders was made real. Such good, important formation and growth.

I believed so much in the power of the short-term mission trip that it was one of the first things I initiated when I became a youth pastor. Casting vision for the importance of building a home for a needy Mexican family and having our youth do the work wasn't a hard sell for my board, teens' parents, or youth ministry volunteers. We would lock it in our calendar, have a parent meeting, raise a ton of money, host weekly mission trip trainings for the teens, and finally gear up to head south of the border. Both churches where I was a youth pastor were in central California, so we'd make the drive to San Diego to stop for one more "normal" meal before heading into Tijuana. Praying our way across the border, it always felt like we needed a little extra of God's favor to safely navigate the potential pitfalls of being out of the United States.

I know I may sound cynical or sarcastic, but this was all actually true of my experience and the many other mission trips I either participated in or led over that decade. We'd get to our basecamp and head out to our work site for the day—and repeat, over and over. One of us would sit with the Mexican family who was receiving the house and ask them to receive Jesus as their personal savior and we'd have an altar call at the VBS we put on each week for local children.

We'd come home with a million stories to share at "Youth Sunday" and statistics for our newsletters, and we'd gear up for the next year.

God had blessed us. Our goal was accomplished. The teenagers got "missions" experience. A poor family got a house. Mexican kids prayed the prayer.

Repeat.

In 2010, two experiences upended my perspective on short-term mission trips and opened my eyes to something very new.

The first was moving to San Diego with my young family to be part of a neighborhood church community. One of the couples in our church spent most of their lives in Mexico before moving to San Diego a couple years earlier. Maria was a Mexican born and raised in Tijuana and her husband, Shaun, was born and raised in the U.S., but had moved to Mexico after meeting Maria. Through our friendship, we quickly discovered that San Diego and Tijuana are one large, binational city completely interdependent politically, economically, relationally, socially, and spiritually. It is the most crossed border in the world and many in the region cross it every morning and evening as part of their work commute.

As we grew in our friendship with Shaun and Maria, they began to introduce us to their Mexican friends in Tijuana…many of whom lived in the very same neighborhoods where I used to pray for safety during my short-term mission trips as a youth pastor. But, for Shaun and Maria this wasn't scary, this was regular life. This was family. These were friends. Being in these relationships was simply what it meant to be a neighbor.

I was already disoriented, but it was Maria sharing her experience as a child in Tijuana that wrecked me. She said that Tijuana was the "most evangelized city in the world" because of its close proximity to wealthy, well-intentioned Christians in southern California who wanted to help the "marginalized" and needed a convenient short-term mission trip, and found that there was no better place than Tijuana. Maria described being a child and watching church groups pull up into her neighborhood in their white vans and prepare for the week's Vacation Bible School. For her and her friends, that meant they were going to get a free week of candy and entertainment…but they knew it'd probably require they "raise their hand" to accept Jesus as their personal savior. Again.

Maria also talked about how toxic the house-building process was for the local community, as some family was "chosen" and everyone around them wasn't. It not only created a culture of dependence, but competition. The local pastor who the U.S. church groups often worked with was given the impossible task of "picking" the family, but everyone knew there were many factors at play that didn't have anything to do with charity. The relational dynamics were destructive.

Maria, like Luis, was healing my sight and forcing me to reconcile my participation in broken systems that were breaking people. I could no longer justify my inherited short-term missions paradigm knowing the impact it had in destabilizing the local community in Tijuana. Through their gracious friendship (they are still dear friends and core staff on our Global Immersion team), Tijuana was no longer dangerous foreign territory, but our backyard full of friends we love. Today, our four little kiddos are as comfortable in Tijuana as they are in San Diego. They are part of a kingdom family that transcends

borders.

The second experience took place on the other side of the globe at the epicenter of one of the most controversial and polarizing conflicts in the world: Israel/Palestine. It not only upended my perspective on short-term mission trips, it gave me a glimpse into alternatives. A shift from *going on a mission trip* to *being shaped for mission* through immersion in uncommon friendships.

The year before this experience, my wife and I had spent a summer living in Jerusalem as I studied the historical context of Jesus at Jerusalem University College. The historical rocks were fascinating, but building relationships with Israelis and Palestinians living in the region was life-changing. Now, a year later, I had the opportunity to go back to the region as a student of Fuller Seminary to study peacemaking from scholars and practitioners who were giving their lives for peace in the context of conflict.

Over the course of two weeks, fellow Fuller students and I sat at the feet of Jews, Christians, and Muslims living some of the most compelling, costly, and tangible expressions of love, forgiveness, and courage I have ever seen. These were not the people or stories that made the headlines, but they were the people who were ushering in a future worth giving our lives to make real. A Jewish mother forgiving the Palestinian who killed her daughter. A Palestinian family whose farm had been destroyed by illegal Israeli settlements who responded by saying, "As followers of Jesus, we refuse to be enemies." One of the world's leading Muslim teachers inviting us to cure our societal disease of Islamophobia by hearing *from* Muslim rather than just *about* them.

Before I went on this trip, many well-intentioned Christian friends assumed I was going on a mission trip to Israel/Palestine to bring peace to the region. When I said I was taking a seminary class in Christian Peacemaking, the immediate assumption was that I was going to "fix" their problem. In reality, though I don't think I would have had words for it back then, they were helping "fix" me. I was being cured of my hero complex and given the gift of friendship.

In this paradigm, the people I was going to visit weren't projects for me to fix, they were my instructors and guides. I was no longer in control and the Spirit was freed to move in ways I had never experienced. It was liberating and terrifying.

On the first day of the trip, I met a fellow Fuller student named Jer Swigart who was also a pastor in a similar season of life. We connected right away and took in most of the experience side by side. We'd process our learnings on the bus between meetings, tell stories of our shared experiences as youth pastors, and cast big visions for what we dreamed our churches might live into when we got home. At one point toward the end of the trip, I remember us saying, "We have to bring people from our churches back here to meet, learn from, and get trained by these remarkable peacemakers we've met the past two weeks."

Within six months, we had put together a group (half from his church and half from mine) of people interested in just that, and within a year we were back in the region, learning from Israelis and Palestinians who were not only our guides but quickly becoming our friends. Early on, we knew we weren't interested in leading mission trips, but we weren't exactly sure what we were leading. It became clear that through this network of uncommon friendships we weren't hosting mission trips—we were creating opportunities for Jesus followers to be trained for mission. We began to say, "the mission trip begins when you land back home."

Eight years later, our organization, The Global Immersion Project, has led immersion trips to Israel/Palestine and San Diego/Tijuana for over a thousand participants, many of whom have been teenagers and college students. We've been invited by our Indigenous peacemaking partners in Israel, Palestine, Tijuana, and San Diego to co-create a new paradigm for "mission trips" that prioritizes uncommon friendships, relational solidarity, personal formation, and long-term missional practice. The "heroes" have become the students and the "projects" have become the lifelong friendships. We trust it is in this posture and practice that God can form us into participants in God's bigger mission of restoration—which is good news for us all.

OUR PRIORITIES

While living for a few months in one of the "young towns" surrounding Lima, Peru, I first heard the term "reverse mission." I had come from the North to the South to help the poor, but the longer I was among the poor the more I became aware that there was another mission, the mission from the South to the North. When I returned to the North, I was deeply convinced that my main task would be to help the poor of Latin America convert their wealthy brothers and sisters in the United States and Canada.

Ever since that time, I have become aware that wherever God's Spirit is present there is a reverse mission. (from *Here and Now* by Henri J.M. Nouwen)

In the next section, I'll get into the specifics of how we structure, guide, and follow up on the formational impact of our immersion trips (which range from three to eight days on the ground), but I want to start by highlighting the formational priorities that are the foundation of how and what we do.

From Mission Trip to Being Shaped *for* Mission

If there is anything we have all learned and experienced, it's that short-term mission trips have a profound impact on the participant. We couldn't agree more and have made that impact our priority. As we began to reflect on the mission trips we had led before launching Global Immersion, there were endless stories of transformation and impact on those of us who were getting in the white buses and heading south of the border. As we on our staff acknowledged that, it inspired us to ask a question: "Wouldn't it show integrity to simply own the fact that these trips are primarily about our own transformation?"

Now, of course there are individuals on the local level who benefit from short-term mission trips (namely those who are getting a new house), but the stories of impact when we get back home were almost always about what *we* learned and how we benefited from the experience. It's time we name what's been true all along: We are the ones getting the best end of this deal as we experience the "reverse mission" Henri Nouwen mentions in the opening quote of this section. God is saving us through the ones we were "sent to go save." The economy of God's kingdom isn't one of power, wealth, and privilege; it's one of humility, sacrifice, and creative love. If that's the case, why would we be surprised that it's the ones on the underside of power and privilege who are saving us from our idols of heroism and self-importance?!

With all that being said, our priority is to create space for our participants (ourselves included!) being "saved," rather than on "saving" the local Indigenous communities. The starting point must be transformation in me, not transformation in them. The question then becomes "How is God shaping me through them?" rather than "How is God shaping them through me?" This question not only forms our posture, it forms our metrics of success. Short-term missions are often project-based with a certain list of objectives. We would argue that *we* are the projects that need to be remade. We will understand the impact of the trip in the way we live upon return back home. The "success" is made real in how we live as transformed followers of Jesus who are committed to participating in God's restorative work (peace) around our tables, on our streets, in our schools, and across the world.

Ellie Roscher is a youth pastor at Bethlehem Lutheran Church in Minnesota whose teens have participated in our organization's immersion trips over the years. I asked her to share reflections on the way this shift from mission trip to formational travel (in other words, travel that shapes us for mission) has played itself out in the lives of her teenagers.

I think the main thing I focus on with youth is identifying the privilege they were born with and helping them see how the system is set up for them to succeed. We go, then, to find Jesus on the margins and to sit, listen, and learn. Then we take what we learned back home to our context, where we have the most power, and we work inside the systems to transform them. I find that focusing this way leads youth to be way more energized and equipped in the long term. They come home ready to know their work—their lifelong work of reconciliation—starts after the trip.

In the old model, the work is done once you get home, and kids go back to the status quo. The mountaintop was contained in the immersion and we have to travel to get that feeling again. By realizing that the real work begins back home, teenagers better understand the messiness of the world, they see the brokenness, and they feel empowered to enter into that as faithful people. Often youth are told they are not powerful yet. They are told to wait.

Our youth identify as peacemakers and know they have time and talent to offer. We have youth lead student walkouts to end gun violence, take Arabic classes, do home stays with families who identify as immigrants, and go to Iftar meals with Muslims. I see them make different decisions about where they go to school, what they study, and what work they want to do. I see them get more curious about their own neighborhoods and their own ancestry. They get more involved in local politics and cross boundaries more boldly and with humility.

In short, this priority moves us from a paradigm of mission trips to formational travel. Immersion into pain, difference, and diversity is actually a reflection of mission in and of itself. There isn't always a good or service to produce, but there is always a posture to embrace that is reflective of God's mission to restore all things. Restoration needs to start in us before we move toward grand visions of restoring others. And, the reality is, we don't have any idea of what working toward someone else's restoration actually looks like until we are in real, genuine relationship with them. Which leads me to our next priority.

From Charity to Solidarity

Despite our best intentions, many short-term mission trips perpetuate a paternalistic paradigm of charity. Throughout modern history, Western Christians often go to the majority world seeking to fix problems with the solutions we have predetermined are best for the local community. We become distributors of goods and services rather than long-term friends who partner with locals in meeting the needs of Indigenous communities.

Samuel Perez has become a close friend and is a full-time teammate of mine at Global Immersion. He is Mexican, lives in Tijuana, and has given his life to standing in solidarity with the migrant and deportee community in his city. Early in our relationship, he boldly invited us to reconsider our understanding of binational relationships by saying, "We don't need your charity, we need your solidarity." Samuel was echoing what Luis had said years before about the harmful impact of short-term mission trips on Tijuana. Rather than Western churches prescribing the answers to the problems of Tijuana, Samuel's words are a reminder to pursue mutual relationships that create space for us to focus instead on partnering together with the local community to meet needs in ways that are actually helpful to the long-term flourishing of those we seek to serve. In short, Samuel encourages taking the time to actually become friends before attempting to "fix" anything.

Rather than going to some far-off country offering humanitarian aid like heart surgeries, we need to enter into friendship with the local community and ask how we can support what God is already doing in that region—and genuinely listen to the response. When we give a premature diagnosis of someone else's "problem," the quick fixes we offer may leave the local community in ruins. We learn more when we take part in genuine, mutual relationships. We may find out that the local community didn't need us to give heart surgeries, they simply needed bandages for skinned knees. When we give something that doesn't meet a community's actual needs and doesn't enter into what they are already doing, in the end they are worse off than when we showed up. Not only does this reflect our hero complex, it undermines trust. This is a human tragedy and antithetical to the gospel.

Moving from charity to solidarity requires us to release the posture of a hero and embrace the posture of a learner. We should not only follow the lead of locals, we must become students of the context and the people who live there. We must do our homework, begin to understand the broken systems that are breaking people, and trust that God is everywhere and already at work. Our job is simply to build relationships with the people who are already at work and join in. The Western Church must repent from an economy of colonization and move to embrace an economy of collaboration.

In 2018, a major influx of migrants from Central America made its way to Tijuana to seek asylum in the United States. Many of these people were fleeing violence in their home countries and had no choice but to migrate north, seeking safety and a future for their children. As our organization observed this phenomenon (one that's not unprecedented throughout history), we listened to our local partners for their view on how we could offer support. Because we had spent years building relationships based in trust, our partners in Tijuana invited us to collaborate in a binational partnership to care for the immediate humanitarian needs of the migrants, leverage our access to resources in order to fund a network of shelters in churches throughout Tijuana, and physically stand with them as a reflection of our long-term, mutual friendship.

That December, our organization invited people of faith from around the United States to come down to Tijuana and learn from local Mexican pastors, humanitarians, activists, and the Central American migrants themselves. We brought the supplies they had requested (sleeping bags, tents, etc.), we shared meals, and we participated in a binational church service at the border wall celebrating a kingdom that transcends borders. It was an experience of the kingdom of God like few of us had ever been part of, and it woke us all up to the holy power of solidarity. Now, as we bring groups in from across the country for our three-day immersion trips, we are inviting people into an ongoing story of God's restorative work that isn't reserved for a mountaintop experience, but a kingdom family that is knit together on a common mission.

Ongoing Discipleship

The paradigm I and those I work with have adopted for short-term missions requires us to care about how we *engage* the experience as much as *what* we experience. Formational travel shapes us because it creates the space for our own discipleship. Rather than simply notice a problem, diagnose from afar, and seek to solve it when we land on the ground, we are given the gift of learning to see the humanity, dignity, and image of God in everyone. We are invited to immerse into the local context, seeking to listen and understand rather than to "preach" and be understood. In the context of long-term relationships, we are invited to roll up our sleeves and contend with each other in costly, creative ways. As we go on this formational discipleship journey, God is able to not only restore what is broken on the ground, but restore what is broken in us.

In the end, this "reverse mission" approach is creating the space for Jesus to heal our sight so we'll begin noticing those we have been taught not to see on our own streets and in our own schools and churches. Fueled by the Spirit and under the instruction of local leaders, we are being commissioned to go back home as ambassadors of a reconciliation (2 Corinthians 5) that was made real in Jesus and continues to be offered to each one of us today. Our work begins when we arrive back home and it likely won't be easy, convenient, or quick. The journey of discipleship never is. Richard Rohr puts it well: "There are two ways of being a prophet. One is to tell the enslaved that they can be free. It is the difficult path of Moses. The second is to tell those who think they are free that they are in fact enslaved. This is the even more difficult path of Jesus."[2]

May we find freedom as we courageously return home and free the enslaved from the captivity they may not even know they are living in.

OUR APPROACH

Before I get tangible about the nuts and bolts of our immersion trips, I need to make a few comments about the heart of the mission these trips pour out of. The mission is the starting point and this way of approaching trips will make more sense with some explication.

Our organization, The Global Immersion Project, is a peacemaking organization that trains people of faith to engage our divided world in restorative ways. We believe the mission of God is restoration and that peacemaking is the vocation of God's people (2 Corinthians 5). In short, from the moment we grabbed for the fruit of power (Genesis 3), God's mission has been to heal and restore what is broken in us and our world. It's clear throughout the story of the Bible that God invites humanity to be active participants in this mission of restoration (Genesis 12). We are all invited to be peacemakers whose lives reflect God's desire to offer a holistic repair of relationships between us and God, us and our neighbor, and us and ourselves. We define peace as the holistic repair of severed relationships.

Viewed this way, peacemaking isn't a clever program or add-on to our faith, it is at the very center of our discipleship journey. Methodologically, we've found there is no better context to teach peace than actual conflict and there are no better instructors than those who are practicing peace in the midst of conflict.

I believe the best way to move forward with short-term missions is to shift from the paradigm of hosting mission trips to training teenagers for mission back home, at their schools and around our world. The rest of this chapter will outline how we do that at our organization.

Dynamic Content

When a group registers for one of our trips, they aren't signing up for a one-off short-term trip, but a transformational journey. Each trip has three phases: the understanding phase, the exposure phase, and the integration phase. The understanding phase is the required learning that happens from five weeks to five months before landing on the ground for the trip. This phase has two core objectives: 1. To establish a theology and practice for everyday peacemaking, and 2. To establish an understanding of the context of the conflict the group will be immersed in during the exposure phase (the immersion trip).

On our organization's trips, the understanding phase (pre-trip learning) is centered around an online course that is a collection of video lectures, articles, videos, documentaries, discussion questions, and group exercises with which each participant is expected to engage. For groups of young people, our staff works closely with the youth pastor/leader/teacher to offer coaching in how to guide their teenagers in and through this content. Most youth ministries make this content the primary focus of their youth gatherings the semester leading up to their trip. They may host separate regular meetings for the participants or integrate the content into their larger curriculum for the entire youth group. Because the youth leader will be the one walking with the teenagers most intimately before and after the trip, it is critical that they take ownership of implementing this phase of learning.

Because we are training young people for mission rather than simply hosting one-off mission trips, we need every participant to build a set of tools to live as peacemakers, and to have a working understanding of the conflict (in our case, these conflicts are in the borderlands of Tijuana/San Diego and Israel/Palestine). It honors our peacemaking partners when participants land on the ground for a trip equipped to ask good questions and embrace a posture of curiosity, and prepared to see this as an opportunity for learning rather than "doing." Every step of the preparation is practical, with the intention of each participant coming out of their learning with very tangible next steps toward their local practice as peacemakers once they return home. I'll get into the next two phases below.

Intentional Displacement

The exposure phase is the immersion trip itself. Our experience is that Christians from the United States need to experience intentional displacement from their normal, everyday lives, which are often insulated from the conflicted realities of our world. Most often, short-term mission trips create opportunities for experientially expanding our worldview, but on these trips participants still take the posture of heroes rather than learners. We have found that intentional displacement with a desire to "serve with" rather than "serve for" is an antidote to our hero complex. It forces us to release control and experience a healthy disorientation that creates space for the Spirit to work in and through us—to open our eyes and hearts to realities and people we have often been taught NOT to see.

While we seek to "disorient" our participants, our team is also committed to guiding groups back to a "reorientation" around the life, teachings, death, and resurrection of Jesus. After every interaction with a local peacemaker, we create space for coaching, discussion, and entering into spiritual practices that root us in a formational journey. We talk with groups about the tension of seeing so much pain and wanting to jump to the quick fixes. We integrate ancient practices like lament that allow us to express our righteous anger in ways that shape us and grow us closer to the heart of God and of other people.

In this exposure phase, we travel far off the beaten paths of tourism or traditional short-term mission trips and enter into the beautiful and broken realities of the local context. On the trips we take to the border, we spend the night in a migrant shelter where we share meals and a roof with people who have recently been deported and others who have been traveling from all over the world to seek asylum in the United States. It's holy ground. We do our best to stay immersed in the context rather than giving in to our inherent privilege and running back to the comforts of home.

As we confront our blind spots and see people and places we normally wouldn't, we ask questions like, "Who have you been taught to see and taught NOT to see back in your school or city?" "What are the barriers that have gotten in the way of seeing the way Jesus sees?" "How might you need Jesus to heal your sight?"

Uncommon Friendships

On our trips, we model the gift of uncommon friendships. Rather than meet only with people we agree with, we create space to learn and hear from people engaging the conflict of the context we find ourselves in from all different angles. On the border, we meet with people including immigration activists, local clergy, Border Patrol agents, deported U.S. military veterans, and Mexican humanitarians. In Israel/Palestine, we meet with Orthodox rabbis living in Jewish settlements in the West Bank, Muslim clerics in Jerusalem, Christian Palestinians living under military occupation, and families who have lost loved ones in the conflict, among others.

Our goal is to create space for our imaginations to be stirred and for us to be moved toward relationship. In a world of binaries (us vs. them), it is a holy disruption to sit with people who "shouldn't" be friends who have decided to partner in a common mission toward restoration. When we share a meal with a Jewish former Israeli Defense Force soldier and a Muslim Palestinian who's given his life to nonviolently fight for the freedom of Palestinians, it's as if the kingdom of God turns 3-D. Former enemies are now friends who are building a future together. That's the stuff of good news! We see that peacemaking doesn't mean a passive withdrawal from conflict or disagreement, but a proactive movement toward them. What if our teenagers, the next generation of Christians in this world of conflict and divide, embraced this posture toward the "other"? In my experience and the experience of those I work with, they desperately want to, but they need leaders to guide them on this path.

Coaching and Collaboration with Youth Workers for Ongoing Formation

After the trip, we enter into what we call the integration phase. It is upon arrival back home that the work really begins. Working closely with youth workers, we build a pathway for long-term transformation and practice. While we are on the trip itself, the youth workers are only responsible for the formation of their teenagers (our team takes care of all the logistics, so the youth workers are focused on pastoring, not event coordination). This frees them up to be present to what is stirring in the lives of their teens. Our team has developed a post-trip curriculum that reinforces what's been learned and mobilizes participants toward missional living locally. Again, the youth worker is the primary guide and we do our best to coach, provide resources for, and encourage their leadership as they translate a one-off "trip" to a formational way of life. It is this phase that ensures we aren't simply facilitating a mountaintop experience, but a discipleship journey that informs everything about the way teenagers live, love, and lead. Some core questions we ask:

- Who have you been taught to see and who have you been taught NOT to see in your neighborhood or at your school? What have been the barriers that have kept you from seeing the humanity, dignity, and image of God in that community?

- What are some tangible ways to learn about this marginalized community and begin to build relationships with them?

- What is a conflict back home (with parents, siblings, friends, etc.) in need of restoration? What is a peacemaking practice you have learned on this trip that you can utilize as a tool to move toward this conflict seeking to heal?

- As you move toward people who may look, think, act, and believe differently than you do, how do you expect your loved ones to respond? What are the spiritual practices that keep you rooted in your identity as God's beloved so you can withstand the critique and concern of those closest to you?

Some core practices we suggest:

- Share about your experience on the immersion trip with your family in a way that highlights your transformation/learnings rather than partisan talking points.

- As you walk down the street, pay attention to what is beautiful and what is broken. Take a picture of both on your smartphone talk about the pictures with a friend.

- Practice seeing the humanity, dignity, and image of God in everyone by looking in the eyes of your neighbors who live outside.

- When you see someone at school being bullied, commit to moving toward the conflict courageously and creatively despite the ways it may impact your reputation.

- As a youth group, become students of your city and those who are doing good work to make peace real. Rather than starting your own program or ministry, choose to be the best volunteers possible.

I asked a youth worker, Ryan Crane, to share some stories of how this formational journey impacted the lives of the teens he works with upon their arrival back home. Ryan is a history and social justice teacher at a Christian high school in the Pacific Northwest who has taken multiple groups of teenagers on our Immigrants Journey immersion trip in San Diego/Tijuana.

As a part of a required twelfth grade course, students vision and propose a plan to make the school community better in ten years. A couple of Immigrants Journey students are using the everyday peacemaking practices to push the school community to rethink its mission trip culture. To step back and consider better practices around pre-trip training, around the WHY of going on a trip and around post-trip integration practices.

I often hear about students bringing the stories of those they met in the borderlands into classroom Socratic seminars, inviting their peers into proximity with those on the underside of power, urging classmates with power in the palms of their hands to leverage that for good.

This generation of teenagers is willing and ready to lean into hard conversations about privilege and power. In fact, our experience is that many demand it if we are to have any credible influence in their lives. These kinds of immersion trips expose the distance many of us have from society's most vulnerable and invite teenagers to consider who and where the vulnerable are in their own context. Far more impactful than a teacher talking about privilege is a peer inviting her classmates into its reality through the context of a shared story. They aren't talking about an esoteric concept that can breed shame, but telling their own story of transformation and inviting their peers to go on the journey with them. Ryan also shared the following:

Social media is a huge platform for young people and ground zero for so much person-to-person engagement. Students who have travelled on Global Immersion trips bring the asset of storytelling into their posts AND into comment threads. Their social media presence can give information and model effective peacemaking practices. I often tell them that even if they can't get the handful of people that are resisting their invitations to consider those on the margins, there is an audience of curious bystanders, who may not be double tapping or commenting, but are watching their advocacy unfold.

Ryan's words here emphasize something important. In today's polarized world where sending the most compelling tweet has a higher social value than living a compelling life, it is critical that teenagers transcend the binaries of social media with a generosity and curiosity that grow trust. Social media is no longer a neutral part of life, it is the very soil in which many relationships are stewarded or shattered. When teenagers gain tools for navigating complexity as conduits of God's restorative work, it is a tangible act of peacemaking in an everyday form.

There are students, many on the brink of college decisions, imagining what incorporating peacemaking looks like into their post-high school plans. Many are considering what it looks like, not to sell everything and move to the borderlands, but to bring the experience of the borderlands and their knowledge of peacemaking to their college campuses, their gap years, and their internships.

Honestly, it would make the most sense to me to tell you stories of a student that upon returning from the trip is now on track to become an immigration lawyer, or moving as soon as possible to the borderlands to be back in the place of their catalytic experience, or mobilize peers to protest at the local detention center. However, what I've found is that students see that their work begins in the places most proximate to them—social media feeds, dinner tables, classroom projects, Bible classes, etc. As they encounter the reality of the depths of their privilege on the borderlands trip, meeting Indigenous peacemakers in that context, they ultimately see their own people and places as the mission field. These are the people on trajectories toward places of power as doctors, lawyers, teachers, business leaders—wondering, what if my investment in my own community was the cultivating of a seed that would grow into these power players leveraging their success for those on the underside of empire?

Oftentimes, the impact of a short-term missions experience gets left behind when crossing the border to head home. Or the impact is so great that teenagers feel like their only choice is to move to the village they served and become full-time missionaries or activists. What if instead of forgetting the experience or taking it on as a laundry list of obligations, our teenagers, like Ryan's, understand that Jesus is inviting them to a way of life that integrates into their college studies, family dynamics, and vocational choices? We aren't forming one-off activists, we are forming disciples who participate in God's mission of restoration in whatever context they inhabit.

FINAL THOUGHTS

However you've experienced these words and stories, please know my primary desire is not to offer another paradigm for short-term mission trips—it's to invite teenagers into a way of life that is shaped by the life, teachings, death, and resurrection of Jesus. We at our organization want to invite young people to participate in God's mission of restoration by embracing their vocation as peacemakers in a divided world. This mission and vocation will inform how they see themselves, read and interpret their Bibles, make decisions about their future, interact with their "other," leverage their inherited privilege for the good of those without, and shape the future of the church.

This is our opportunity to take seriously our sacred role of guiding the next generation into a faith that's worth their lives. As I reflect on my own formation, I've had to spend years unraveling the toxic view of Christianity and missions I had inherited from my well-intentioned evangelical leaders. What if we not only save our teenagers a decade of unlearning, but also offer them a message and mission that could remake the world in ways reflective of the Jesus we follow?

As ones who have been at the epicenter of the short-term missions "problem," and been on a long, painful journey of confession and repentance, those who are part of my organization understand ways this message may sound overly critical or disorienting. While we hope it doesn't lead toward shame, we do hope it creates space to ask hard, costly questions and outline a framework that could lead us down a path toward healing. The collective witness of the church is at stake, and we have the opportunity to hand off the baton of this witness to a generation that is growing familiar with the global family that is the broader church.

In a globalized world, the next generation is not only more aware of the impact of bad theology and practice than ever before (and is leaving traditional structures of "church" as a result), they are energized to embrace their identity as global citizens. Teenagers need to know they are first and foremost members of a kingdom family, a family that transcends borders, race, and culture. It's time we stop inviting them to an unsatisfying (and unhealthy) drive-thru and instead invite them to a family reunion around the table of a global feast. It's time they hear the story and learn from their great-uncles, great-aunts, grandmas, and grandpas. There is so much wisdom, shared humanity, and story we have kept from our teenagers, and I have to imagine these immersion trips are the fireside conversations where the Spirit is freed to move, breathe, and mobilize the next generation for lives of mission, every moment of every day.

May it be so.

RESPONSE

TODD FRENEAUX

Jon has some good stuff here and his heart for peacemaking comes through loud and clear. I love the concept of "shaping people for mission" and believe this is an important piece as we seek to effectively prepare the hearts and minds of those desiring to serve. In particular, the "understanding phase" is so vital as that first step. It gets me thinking about how youth groups can take a similar approach and do a better job of preparing their youth before engaging them in a traditional short-term mission trip.

I also agree that ministry is more effective when we build relationships and partner with the community to meet their needs, rather than just becoming "distributors of goods and services," as Jon suggests. Personally, I am a champion of this approach. I have witnessed the benefits of putting a priority on relationships and have seen that play out in significant ways in my own context, serving three communities on an ongoing basis.

I also agree wholeheartedly that the practices of some traditional short-term missions organizations are problematic and can do more harm than good. It's unfortunate that Jon has participated with organizations that have left him, and undoubtedly many others, disappointed and questioning the validity of short-term mission trips altogether. But before we throw traditional short-term mission trips under the proverbial church bus, let's consider a few thoughts.

First, let's be clear that Jon offers a different approach to missions, but not necessarily a better one. The goals his organization strives for are quite different from the goals that accompany many traditional approaches to short-term missions, including mine. His organization places a high priority on peacemaking. That's good. But another organization may emphasize serving and ministering to the needs of the homeless. That's good, too. Still another may place a high priority on ministering to the incarcerated. I believe that God desires to use a variety of ministries and organizations to accomplish his will and advance his kingdom, and he does that through both traditional short-term mission trips and non-traditional approaches to mission.

Second, when Jon writes of peacemaking, I can't help but wonder if it's more about acceptance, tolerance, and agreement with others than it is about introducing Jesus to them once a relationship has been established. The approach feels a little bit like, "can't we all just get along?" If, as Christ-followers, we are only building relationships, helping people, and being peacemakers, then what distinguishes us from just being good people doing good things?

I also find the assertion that peacemaking "is at the very center of our discipleship journey" to be concerning. I would submit that the center of our discipleship journey should be based on our total commitment to Jesus Christ. From here the fruits of the Spirit will be manifested (love, joy, peace…). Peacemaking is then a result of a relationship with Jesus because that relationship is what will ultimately fuel and sustain a person's passion to be a true peacemaker for the kingdom of God. 2 Corinthians 5:18 makes it clear that we must first be reconciled to God before we can have the ministry of reconciliation with others.

Lastly, Jon states that the real beneficiaries of traditional short-term mission trips are the participants, and that we should own that. I would argue that both the giver and the receiver can benefit equally. Clearly, we want to establish relationships and meet the needs of those we are serving, but the hope is that teens are encountering the living Lord and being shaped for mission in the midst of serving others. If we do this right, we are developing youth into servant leaders for a lifetime. Could we do more to prepare and shape them before going into the mission field? Absolutely.

Writing as someone who has been on the front lines of traditional short-term missions work for more than twenty years, I can assure you that the short-term missions "problem" that Jon speaks of has transformed countless lives in significant ways on both sides of the mission. Let's recognize and celebrate the many ways we successfully engage teens in short-term missions and avoid those organizations that fail to bear fruit for the kingdom of God.

APPENDIX

The Importance of Engaging Junior Highers in Short-Term Missions | Todd Freneaux

It was our fall junior high retreat weekend in the Catoctin Mountains of Maryland, a beautiful setting for what would become one of the most memorable retreat experiences of my life.

I was in my twenties, volunteering alongside my mentor (and volunteer junior high leader), Doug. Doug's passion for junior high youth was infectious. "There is no better age," he would often say. His eyes would light up and his smile would grow big every time he talked about ministry with junior highers. I, too, fell in love with this amazing age group.

On Saturday night, Doug had planned to do a foot washing. I know what you're thinking. "A foot washing with junior high kids? Why? That's just a train wreck waiting to happen." Well, to tell you the truth, I was too young to be concerned. Besides, I trusted Doug, and he was confident that it was the right thing to do with this group.

The carpeted room we sat in jutted out over the lake. About thirty chairs were set up in a circle. The room was lit only by candles, with a basin of water and some towels placed in the center of the circle. After everyone was seated, Doug proceeded to share about the night Jesus washed his disciples' feet. Doug was a great storyteller and the youth were uncharacteristically quiet, hanging on to his every word.

A few minutes later, the foot washing began. It started slowly at first, but then one by one, youth and adult leaders came to the center of the circle, picked up the basin and a towel, and began to wash one another's feet. Some junior highers who had only washed one or two others' feet went back again to wash the feet of ones they'd missed. Silence. Tears. Holy Spirit.
At one point, a boy who had cerebral palsy made his way to the basin,

clumsily. We looked on as he proceeded to wash *every* person's feet, methodically moving around the circle. His physical challenges made it painful to watch as he struggled to move from one person to the next. If there was a dry eye before he began, there wasn't one after he finished.

At some point I glanced at my watch and realized this had been going on for two hours. Two hours? I was amazed.

When everyone had finished, Doug closed our time together. There wasn't much to say, really. That night, the room was filled with God's presence to a degree that I had never experienced before. I will never, ever forget it.

Later that evening as I reflected on our time together, I was a bit confused. Was this the same group of boys who bounced off the walls every week at youth group and refused to settle down, despite our best efforts and threats? And was this the same group of girls who were backstabbing each other a few weeks ago by saying some of the most hurtful things they could to one another?

How could these junior high youth be capable of what happened tonight in that room?

I'm not sure who coined the phrase, but it has stuck with me for decades: *"Junior highers are capable of everything—and nothing—at the same time."* How true. What I experienced and witnessed on that retreat, coupled with many similar experiences, had a profound impact on me and shaped my view of junior high ministry.

Why Not Junior High?
Fast forward about a dozen years. I was the full-time director of youth ministries in a large United Methodist church in Williamsburg, VA. After three years in my position, I had become increasingly frustrated with the fact that there were so very few missions organizations providing a mission trip experience designed for sixth, seventh, and eighth graders. For the most part, the organizations that *did* allow junior highers to participate were simply not able to effectively

program for two age groups. Clearly, their target age group was senior high.

Why was that? After all, when we have numbers to support it—we provide separate programing for junior high youth in our youth group for weekly events, retreat weekends, and special activities. And we rarely, if ever, combine junior high and senior high in our small groups. We all know there is a massive difference on so many levels between a sixth grader and an eleventh grader and that it just makes sense to provide separate programming for each age group.

After twenty-plus years of doing mission trips with junior high youth through the Jeremiah Project, I can tell you that engaging them in missions at this critical age has a profound impact on shaping them in the present and establishing a growing commitment to service, to their relationship with Jesus, and to the church.

The message junior highers hear so much of the time is "You're too young to do this or that" or "When you get older, you can [fill in the blank]." As a parent of three girls I know there are things that they must wait till they're older to do. And that's okay. But as the church, we haven't done a very good job of telling our junior high youth that they are at the *perfect age* and *not* too young for God to use them—right here, and right now.

I love the exchange the prophet Jeremiah has with God in Jeremiah 1:4-8 (NCV):

> *The Lord spoke his word to me, saying: "Before I made you in your mother's womb, I chose you. Before you were born, I set you apart for a special work. I appointed you as a prophet to the nations."*
>
> *Then I said, "But Lord God, I don't know how to speak. I am only a boy."*
>
> *But the Lord said to me, "Don't say, 'I am only a boy.' You must go everywhere I send you, and you must say everything I tell you to say. Don't be afraid of anyone, because I am with you to protect you," says the Lord.*

We have an amazing opportunity for a teachable moment with our youth about the power of God in their lives. Wouldn't it be wonderful if we as the church would come alongside our junior high youth and say, *"The world will tell you that you're too young to do a lot of things, but when it comes to the things of God, that's a totally different story. God still calls 'Jeremiahs' today. God believes in you and calls you to be the hands and feet of Christ today."* That's a powerful truth that young people need to hear time and time again.

The reason this is so important is because we know that the early adolescent years (roughly ages eleven to thirteen) represent one of the most significant periods of change in the life of a human. During these years young people are beginning to ask significant soul-searching questions: "Who am I?" "How am I unique?" "How do I, or my choices, matter?" "Where, and to whom, do I belong?"

In light of this truth, we must consider the significant contribution mission trips can have in the lives of young teens during these critical years of development. By engaging junior highers in mission, we are providing a unique setting that allows them to directly explore the very areas of adolescence they are beginning to work out.

Belonging

Young people desperately want to belong. Mission trips provide great opportunities for junior highers to experience what it means to belong to a faith community, which is unlike anything the world can offer. With Christ at the center of this unique community, young teens and adults from all over the state, the country, and the world come together to become the hands and feet of Christ to bring about change and to advance the kingdom of God. Wow! What young person wouldn't want to belong to that?! The earlier youth can discover a sense of their purpose the better, because living into that purpose meets a very real and present developmental need, establishing early on the desire to belong to *this* community.

Uniqueness

We all want our lives to matter. It's no different with junior highers. They are beginning to ask what their unique contribution is. And so, when a young teen gets a taste at an early age of what it's like to really make a difference in the world, they are profoundly impacted by it. Their ability to see why their life matters becomes much easier while on a mission trip. It's life-changing for a junior higher to look back on their missions week and be able to say, "I helped build those steps!" or, "My team built a wheelchair ramp that made it possible for an elderly woman to leave her home for the first time in nine months." The image of that frail woman making her way down the ramp and breaking into a smile will be forever etched in that young person's mind. And somewhere in the deep recesses of his developing brain, he realizes that his life *does* matter and that he *can* contribute something unique.

Identity

This one has many layers and there's certainly not enough space to peel them all back here. The big question junior highers are asking is, "Who am I?" The most critical part of the answer, in my opinion, comes from young teens understanding that their identity is found in Christ, and Christ alone.

Our identity in Christ stands in stark contrast to a world that bombards us every minute with lies that who you are is based on image: the clothes you wear, the electronics you own, the social media presence you put forth, and the list goes on and on.

Although their identities were forming long before middle school, they are now entering new territory: junior highers are beginning to engage in abstract thinking and, in addition to making many other discoveries, are figuring out that the choices they make will have an impact on the person they will become. This is huge! On mission trips, we have an opportunity to impact young teens in the midst of their identity-forming process. How cool is that?

Engaging junior high youth consistently in short-term mission trips helps them form their values, allows them to empathize with the needs of others, expands their worldview, and teaches them to look beyond themselves and realize that their lives and the lives of those around them have value. What a wonderful way to help junior highers discover their identities in Christ.

FINAL THOUGHTS

I work almost exclusively with junior highers, and every summer
I hear over and over from adults that they had no idea junior high
youth were capable of so much. This realization comes in part
because we believe in the youth and tell them that God wants to use
them this week in ways they never imagined. Those are empowering
words that echo in the ears of youth all week long.

We as the church need to dispel the myth that junior highers are too
young for the responsibilities and challenges of a week of mission,
and realize the significant impact these trips have on shaping them
during these formative years. We need to communicate to young
teens early and often that serving God is an adventure. What better
place to be than on a mission trip where they come face to face with
the needs of the real world, serve like Jesus did, and leave knowing
that, just like the prophet Jeremiah, they are not too young to be used
by God.

APPENDIX

The Massive Win of Multigenerational Short-Term Missions | Shawn Kiger

I'm a big believer in short-term mission trips. Attending mission trips with my youth group is how I got interested in youth ministry as a calling when I was in high school. I have taken youth on mission trips for over twenty years and I led a short-term missions program for five years. This book has listed all of the great reasons we in youth ministry should support mission trips. These trips get youth out of their comfort zones, which helps bring transformation to their lives. That's what I experienced and what helped transform my life way back when I was in high school.

But for the last ten years or so I've started to feel that these experiences could be even more powerful if the trips were multigenerational. For years I tried to accomplish that, but those trips mainly became youth trips with a large number of adult volunteers and/or parents. Don't get me wrong, those were still great trips, but it wasn't exactly what I had hoped for.

The last five years, though, I have been taking teams from my church to Haiti. These trips have been what I envisioned when I was looking for true multigenerational short-term mission trips. Each of these experiences has included about half youth and half adults, but the adults attending have not been just youth volunteers or parents. We had some of that, but most of the adults had no past experience with the youth ministry. Most of them were very active in the church, but they were active mostly in adult ministries. They would recognize the youth when they saw them in church, but very few knew any teenager by name. The cool thing about these trips is that they have helped transform not only those who attended them, but they have had a big impact on transforming our entire church.

In youth ministry we have heard for years the dangers that we face by segregating ourselves from the church as a whole. But this doesn't just happen in youth ministry. The entire church does this. There is children's ministry, youth ministry, adult Sunday school, women's ministries, men's ministries, and on and on. We compartmentalize ourselves into groups. I'm not saying that is always a bad thing. Powerful ministry happens in each of those groups, but there is so much we miss out on when we only do ministry that way. That's why I have found that multigenerational short-term mission trips are so beneficial to the overall mission of the church. Multigenerational STMs break down the barriers of siloed ministries.

During our first trip to Haiti I was a little worried that we had half youth and half adults, most of whom have never worked with youth before. I was concerned that the adults would be annoyed with the youth or that the youth would just let the adults talk during sharing time. The first day of the trip proved me wrong. The age group barriers were broken down almost immediately. Part of it could have been because we were in Haiti and, with the exception of myself, it was everyone's first time with an international mission trip. A bond happens quickly when everyone is stretched outside of their comfort zone. Not all the adults could physically play the games the youth were playing, but they tried and the youth quickly included them. The adults even taught the youth new games.

Just as we have heard the dangers of having siloed youth ministries, we have also heard of the important role adults play in adolescent faith development. We know how important the role of parents is in a teenager's faith, but we also know how important it is for teenagers to have other adults who know them by name. Multigenerational mission trips help that to happen in a very short period of time. Because experiences happen at a faster rate on mission trips, the bonds that are created can last a long time. Shared experiences create bonds like nothing else does.

We know that sharing one's beliefs is important for faith development. That happens more naturally during mission trips because we are all living in community together. The beauty of multigenerational mission trips is that not only do youth share their faith, but they get to hear adults share theirs. They get to hear adults they know from church talk about the importance of their faith, their struggles with doubt, and the questions they have. Teenagers then see that they are not the only ones with doubts or questions. This also has a huge impact on the adults. Many times adults only hear negative things about teenagers, but those stereotypes disappear when they see young people caring for others and hear them share their faith.

The overall mission benefits from the more diverse group as well. On youth-only mission trips, when the youth arrive in the community where we are working, there is usually a quick and easy bond between our youth and the younger kids in that community. But when we bring different generations of people, they are able to build relationships among different generations in the community. Parents build relationships with parents, senior adults with senior adults, and so on. We better represent the church, and the kingdom of God, when we have many generations present. The community we are working with notices that as well. Having a diverse group of ages and experiences better equips us for whatever the mission is. Building deeper relationships with people happens more easily with a variety of ages represented and present.

The other huge benefit to our multigenerational Haiti mission trips has been how our entire church has embraced the mission. When we return from our trips, it's not only the youth who share with the congregation about the experience. We still have a Sunday where the youth share. I believe it's important for their faith development and the church's. But having adults come back and share with their adult groups has created a huge buy-in to the mission. Now these adults, some of whom were skeptical of the importance of youth mission trips, have friends who have participated on trips and brought back pictures and shared stories. Our entire church now feels that Haiti is one of our main missions, which would not be the case if it was a youth-only trip. This has been beneficial for how much money we raise and who decides to go. Adults who wondered, often out loud, why we were going to Haiti when there is need in our county are now signing up to go to Haiti. This same support would not happen if it was a youth- or adult-only trip. The transfer of wisdom between the different age groups results in benefits for every part of the mission and the church.

If you are interested in leading a multigenerational mission trip, there are a few things I have learned over the past several years that I think you should consider. You have to be clear in your advertising for the trip that it is open to youth and adults. It does no one any good to be surprised. Having pre-trip meetings is crucial to the trip's success. I have always thought these were important for youth trips, but they are even more important for multigenerational trips. Those meetings are good opportunities for the team to get to know each other and they also provide a good time to stress expectations.

Flexibility is critical for every mission trip, which can sometimes be harder for adults than for youth. Patience and an understanding that everyone has something to add are also important. Every team member is valuable and all have gifts and talents that are important to the mission. If a building project is involved I often have to remind the adults, especially those with a building background, to remember to be patient with the youth and to use the opportunity to teach someone a new skill. Sometimes adults, and some youth, focus so much on the project that they miss out on the experience. The experience is as important as the project—if not more. The shared experience between a youth and an adult transforms the way they think about each generation and how they see their faith.

I often think that youth trips are so much easier, and we do still have youth mission trips, but the extra work it takes to pull off a multigenerational short-term mission trip is completely worth it. There have been times in Haiti when I've looked around to see youth, young adults, parents, grandparents, and other adults (who are not connected in any way to the youth ministry) all together, sharing a meal or talking about the day, and I think this must be what the kingdom of God feels like. It's a beautiful thing!

NOTES

Developing Long-Term Partnerships with Indigenous Church Leaders | Jim Noreen

1. Esteban Ortiz-Ospina, Diana Beltekian, and Max Roser, "Trade and Globalization," ourworldindata.org (website), last revised October 2018, https://ourworldindata.org/trade-and-globalization.

Approaching Urban Missions as Life-Long Learners, Advocates, and Allies | Susie Gamez

1. Jackie Hill Perry's Facebook page. Accessed September 26, 2019. https://www.facebook.com/jackiehillperrypage/posts/1866912776658181.

2. Brian Thompson, "The Racial Wealth Gap: Addressing America's Most Pressing Epidemic," Forbes.com (website), February 18, 2018, https://www.forbes.com/sites/brianthompson1/2018/02/18/the-racial-wealth-gap-addressing-americas-most-pressing-epidemic/#6881bee67a48.

3. National Center for Children in Poverty, "Poverty By the Numbers," nccp.org (website), http://www.nccp.org/media/releases/release_34.html.

4. Cornel West, *Race Matters* (Boston: Beacon Press, 2001).

5. Pew Research Center, "The High Schools Hispanics Attend," pewresearch.org (website), November 1, 2005, https://www.pewresearch.org/hispanic/2005/11/01/the-high-schools-hispanics-attend/.

6. Eileen Patten, "Racial, gender wage gaps persist in U.S. despite some progress," pewresearch.org (website), July 1, 2016, https://www.pewresearch.org/fact-tank/2016/07/01/racial-gender-wage-gaps-persist-in-u-s-despite-some-progress/.

7. For more on these topics, these are two great resources: https://www.huffpost.com/entry/16-books-about-race-that-every-white-person-should-read_n_565f37e8e4b08e945fedaf49 and https://

www.answerpoverty.org/single-post/2016/11/02/Poverty-Race-Faith.

8. James C. Cobb, "When Martin Luther King Jr. was killed, he was less popular than Donald Trump is today," usatoday. com (website), April 4, 2018, https://www.usatoday.com/ story/opinion/2018/04/04/martin-luther-king-jr-50-years-assassination-donald-trump-disapproval-column/482242002/.

9. Jemar Tisby, "Why so many white churches resisted Martin Luther King Jr.'s call," washingtonpost.com (website), January 15, 2018, https://www.usatoday.com/story/opinion/2018/04/04/ martin-luther-king-jr-50-years-assassination-donald-trump-disapproval-column/482242002/.

10. Learn more about the history of South Central LA at southcentralhistory.com.

11. Learn more about the history of gangs in South Central Los Angeles at https://www.pbs.org/independentlens/cripsandbloods/ timeline.html.

12. Bryant Myers, *Walking with the Poor* (Maryknoll, NY: Orbis Books, 1999).

13. This quote of Gideon Yung comes from a blog written by Scott Bessenecker, an InterVarsity Missions Director. Scott Bessenecker, "The Cost of Short Term Missions," urbana.org (website), July 14, 2009, https://urbana.org/blog/cost-short-term-missions.

Alleviating Privilege through Short-Term Missions | Kurt Rietema

1. Brian M. Howell, *Short-Term Mission: An Ethnography of Christian Travel Narrative and Experience* (Westmont, IL: InterVarsity Press, 2012).

2. W.V. Taylor, "Short-Term Missions: Reinforcing Beliefs and Legitimating Poverty," Master's Thesis, University of Tennessee—Knoxville, 2012.

3. *Our Planet*, Netflix nature documentary narrated by David Attenborough and produced by Alastair Fothergill, Keith Scholey,

and Colin Butfield, 2019, https://www.netflix.com/title/80049832.

4. Susan Sontag, *Regarding the Pain of Others* (New York: Picador, 2004).

5. Frederick Douglass, *The Life and Times of Frederick Douglass: From 1817-1882* (London: Christian Age Office, 1882).

6. Shane Claiborne, *The Irresistible Revolution: Living as an Ordinary Radical* (Grand Rapids, MI: Zondervan, 2006).

7. "A Trump Supporter Finds a Surprising Ally at an Anti-Trump Rally," Storycorps.org (website), https://storycorps.org/stories/a-trump-supporter-finds-a-surprising-ally-at-an-anti-trump-rally/. (This story originally aired September 28, 2018, on NPR's Morning Edition.)

From Charity to Solidarity: Decolonizing Short-Term Missions | Jon Huckins

1. Henri J.M. Nouwen, *Here and Now: Living in the Spirit* (New York: The Crossroad Publishing Company, 1994).

2. Richard Rohr, *From Wild Man to Wise Man: Reflections on Male Spirituality* (Cincinnati, OH: Franciscan Media, 2005).

BIOS

Mark Oestreicher is a partner in The Youth Cartel, which provides resources, training, and coaching for church youth workers, and is the author of many books for youth workers, parents, and teenagers. Twitter: @markosbeard.

Todd Freneaux Before he co-founded the Jeremiah Project, Todd Freneaux's goal was to make a living writing country music. He still thinks he should've been born a Wild West cowboy, believing to this day he was born in the wrong year. He serves as the Jeremiah Project's Executive Director (www.jeremiahproject.org), where he lives out his passion for mission, ministry, and leadership development with middle and high school students. He lives with his family in Williamsburg, VA, where his impressive collection of cowboy hats is displayed.

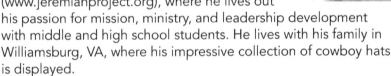

Susie Gamez is Canadian by birth, Korean by heritage, Mexican by marriage, and American by immigration. She is passionate about matters surrounding reconciliation, justice, and the gospel. Susie and her husband, Marcos, met at Fuller Theological Seminary while each of them was getting an M.A. in Intercultural Studies; they now have four beautiful LatAsian babies. After serving as a youth pastor and church planter in South Central Los Angeles for fourteen years, Susie now lives in Long Beach, CA, where she serves on staff with Light and Life Christian Fellowship.

Jon Huckins is the Co-Founding Director of The Global Immersion Project, a peacemaking training organization helping people of faith engage our divided world in restorative ways. He co-leads an intentional Christian community in his neighborhood of Sherman Heights in San Diego and has a master's degree from Fuller Theological Seminary.

Jon is married to Jan and is a dad of four kids, a speaker, and a writer. His latest book is *Mending the Divides: Creative Love in a Conflicted World*. Find Jon at jonhuckins.net, Twitter, or Facebook.

Shawn Kiger is the Director of Youth and Missions at Wright's Chapel UMC in Ladysmith, VA. He has been in youth ministry for over twenty years and is a certified youth ministry coach through The Youth Cartel. He and his wife, Nikki, have two daughters and a St. Bernard.

Jim Noreen is a non-profit leader, focusing exclusively on effective short-term missions through a local church partnership model. Jim serves on the leadership team at Praying Pelican Missions and lives with his wife and four kids in the suburbs of Minneapolis.

Kurt Rietema is the Director of Justice Initiatives at Youthfront and lives and works in a diverse, under-resourced neighborhood of Kansas City. His work includes youth social entrepreneurship, short-term mission, community development, and creating just housing and lending partnerships for immigrants.